Rachael Roberts Joanne Gakonga Andrew Preshous

IELTS Foundation

Teacher's Book

MACMILLAN

Macmillan Education
Between Towns Road, Oxford OX4 3PP
A division of Macmillan Publishers Limited
Companies and representatives throughout the world

ISBN 1 405 01395 8

Designed by Mike Cryer, eMC Design; www.emcdesign.org.uk
Typeset by EXPO Holdings
Illustrated by Oxford Designers & Illustrators
Cover design by Andrew Oliver

Dictionary extracts taken from the *Macmillan Essential Dictionary for Learners
of English* © Bloomsbury Publishing Plc 2003

The publishers would like to thank Celia Bingham for all her hard work on
this project.

Printed and bound in Spain by Edelvives

2008 2007 2006 2005 2004
10 9 8 7 6 5 4 3 2

Introduction

Large numbers of overseas students wish to study at universities and colleges in Britain, Canada and Australasia and the demand for and awareness of IELTS continues to rise.

Many students are aiming for IELTS from a relatively early stage in their studies, but starting at perhaps Band 4–5, find much of the material initially too demanding. This course takes into account the needs of a typical learner (within the approximate 4–6 band range) planning to do IELTS and the particular demands of this test.

IELTS Foundation consists of the following components:

Student's Book
Teacher's book
Cassettes/CD
Study Skills Book

Coursebook

IELTS Foundation is a coursebook that supports the needs of lower level students by offering comprehensive, step-by-step practice within 12 interesting topic-based units. This book takes a systematic approach in preparing overseas students for the Speaking, Listening and Academic Reading and Writing modules of the IELTS exam by providing tips, exam strategies and appropriate practice activities. The suggested time to cover this course is 120 hours, but depending on the level of the students, this could quite easily be shortened or expanded.

The contents are closely based on the IELTS exam assessment criteria and each of the 12 units integrates the four skills thus providing balance and variety. The book also aims to give a thorough grounding in the type of skills necessary to study and perform effectively in an English-speaking academic environment and active learning is encouraged. Therefore, *IELTS Foundation* combines two key elements: IELTS preparation and essential study skills.

To complement these elements, relevant language sections are also integrated into the units to support the learners in developing the necessary accuracy and range, as well as providing them with useful phrases and key lexical items for use in an IELTS context and later in an academic context. Some understanding of discourse, including avoiding repetition and lexical links, is included, and major elements of pronunciation are also considered.

There are also additional appendices on Grammar, Vocabulary and Writing (model answers and comments). For a detailed description of each unit see Contents on pages 2 and 3.

The Teacher's Book

The Teacher's Book provides keys to exercises, including line references indicating where answers to reading text questions are to be found, clear teaching notes for every activity in the Student's Book and guidelines and ideas for exploiting the coursebook material. The Teacher's Book is a very useful guide for those who may be less experienced in this particular area, as it gives comprehensive information about the IELTS exam and the strategies and techniques necessary to achieve a good grade. In addition, it also offers insights into English for Academic Purposes (EAP) particularly the crucial role that study skills play. Tapescripts with highlighted answers are included as well as a number of suggestions for optional activities that can be used to supplement the core materials in the Student's Book. At the back of the Teacher's Book are an extra 12 photocopiable practice activities, each relating to a unit of the book.

Study Skills Book

The Study Skills Book can be used for self-study or as an intensive IELTS preparation course. It is divided into four sections to give further practice in the Speaking, Listening, Academic Reading and Writing modules for the IELTS exam. This workbook includes relevant exercises, sample answers and useful strategies on how to be successful in the IELTS exam. Keys and comments for activities are provided and it also contains a full IELTS practice exam. The Study Skills Book could be used to supplement *IELTS Foundation* or as a separate course.

Core skills areas

A summary of the rationale and basic approach taken for each of the core skills areas is provided below:

Reading

Students at this level may find IELTS reading texts too dense to engage with, which prevents them from developing the necessary skills and techniques. The reading material in *IELTS Foundation* is designed to be accessible and to have a broad appeal to students from a variety of backgrounds and cultures. Texts have been taken from a variety of sources, including newspaper and magazine articles and internet websites as well as academic texts.

In each Reading skills section, the student is given guidance in both understanding the text and in learning to deal with the full range of IELTS question types. Skills such as skimming, scanning, finding topic sentences and guessing the meaning of new vocabulary from context are developed through a series of tasks and students are also given support and useful tips for tackling each type of question. The level of difficulty and length of the texts increases gradually over the course of the book. Note that in the IELTS exam they will have 20 minutes for each text.

Writing

Many lower level learners do not have the linguistic resources available to produce the kind of answers required in the IELTS Writing module. They may also be unfamiliar with the type of writing expected. These difficulties often result in them producing texts that display an inappropriate style or content, lack organization or contain basic linguistic weaknesses.

IELTS Foundation adopts a step-by-step approach that takes lower level learners carefully through each stage of the writing process relating to IELTS Task 1 and 2. Collaborative activities to raise awareness, prepare students and practise key writing skills are provided at each stage. Features focussed on include planning, paragraphing, useful language, style and editing. All units also contain an IELTS Writing question to give individual practice.

As well as focusing on the writing process, a product approach is also adopted by basing tasks on model or authentic student writing. This gives insights into the type of texts required and the level of language that is desirable. These sample answers also develop students' ability to evaluate their own work more closely. Relevant language is highlighted and tasks are often complemented by grammar or vocabulary exercises which also help to improve their writing. Model answers and comments are provided in the Writing section on pages 160–165 of the Student's Book.

Speaking

IELTS Foundation provides guidance and strategies on how to approach the Speaking module. There are numerous opportunities to practise all three parts of the module on a range of topics. Peer and teacher feedback, as well as self-evaluation, are drawn upon to help develop speaking skills. Recordings and tapescripts of authentic student responses are also used for activities and analysis.

To improve students' speaking skills in general, there are regular opportunities to speak in pairs, for example, in pre- and post- reading and listening activities. In addition, language sections throughout the book provide useful words and phrases relating to particular functions such as giving and justifying opinions. Motivating tasks and interesting topics also allow students to present information and ideas or discuss key issues. These types of activities will be useful preparation for future academic contexts.

Listening

Many students at lower levels find listening quite challenging, particularly when texts include more academic vocabulary and are extended monologues, such as lectures as in the final part of the IELTS Listening module. Hearing a text only once, as is the case with IELTS, can also cause difficulty. *IELTS Foundation* gives students practice in all four parts of the Listening module, as well as providing support and useful tips for tackling different question types. In addition, there are further listening activities designed to practise such skills as note taking and listening and writing simultaneously.

Tapescripts are provided on pages 166–175 of the Student's Book for easy reference and also in the Teacher's Book, where answers to questions are clearly marked. This book also gives clear guidance on how to develop students' listening skills by focussing on key areas such as prediction.

Language focus

The language focus sections have two major aims: to improve the level of accuracy by focusing on areas which commonly cause difficulty, and to develop the student's range by introducing more variety of expression.

The language work is integrated into the skills work, often highlighted in a reading or listening text. Students are thus encouraged to 'notice' language in context and to try to formulate rules for themselves before going on to use the language in IELTS Speaking or Writing tasks. Further practice of discrete language areas is provided in a Grammar section on pages 150–154 of the Student's Book.

Vocabulary

The topic-based units help the students to build up key vocabulary around such typical IELTS topics as the environment, health and crime. They are also encouraged to increase the communicative quality of their speaking and writing by learning and using fixed lexical chunks, such as *There is no doubt that…* . In addition, every unit contains a Dictionary focus section, which highlights useful academic words contained within the unit, encouraging the students to notice such language in context, and to start to widen their own lexical range. Finally, the Vocabulary section on pages 155–159 of the Student's Book contains a range of extra activities, focusing on such areas as word affixation and collocation.

Pronunciation

Pronunciation is an area that is often neglected in IELTS material, but which, nonetheless, is important. It is a key component of the IELTS Speaking module and, for many lower level learners, an area that is worthy of attention. *IELTS Foundation* contains regular pronunciation sections which cover a wide range of key issues such as word and sentence stress, intonation and connected speech. These activities are integrated into the units, allowing students opportunities for relevant practice.

Study skills

Focused exam preparation and practice may not always be enough for students to achieve success at IELTS. At lower levels, a solid grounding in study skills is vital in helping them to develop and improve other areas.

Each of the 12 units in *IELTS Foundation* focuses on a particular study skill. The activities and advice provided in these sections will help students develop more effective learning strategies. There is a particular emphasis on 'good learner' habits, reviewing and evaluating work and learning independently in order to use non-classroom time as productively as possible.

The IELTS Exam

IELTS, or the International English Language Testing System, is an exam designed to assess a learner's level of English, on a scale from 1–9 (see page 6 for details). A summary of each module is outlined below:

Listening

Content: This module is in four sections, which get progressively more difficult and takes about 40 minutes. The first two sections are based around social situations. Section 1 will be a conversation between two speakers, such as a conversation between a student and their landlord. Section 2 will be a monologue (one speaker) on a subject of general interest, such as a welcoming speech

for new members of a sports club. The next two sections are more closely related to education or training contexts. Section 3 will be a conversation between two to four people, such as a seminar in which a group of students discuss a topic. Section 4 will be another monologue, such as a lecture, or a talk.

Question Types: There are forty questions in total, ten for each section. Different question types include multiple choice, completing notes or sentences, completing or labelling diagrams, charts or tables, classifying, matching and writing short answers.

Exam Tips: Each section is heard ONCE. However, there is time to look briefly at the questions before each part is played. During the exam, students should write on the question paper, and at the end of the exam have 10 minutes to transfer answers to the answer sheet. It is important they do this carefully, and check grammar and spelling, as mistakes will lose marks.

Academic reading

Content: The exam lasts one hour and there are three reading texts, of increasing difficulty, taken from newspapers, magazines, books and journals. The topics are of general interest, so students do not have to be experts in the subject area to understand them.

Question Types: There are forty questions in total. Question types include multiple choice, choosing *True/ False/Not given*, or *Yes/No/Not given*; identifying the view of the writer; completing sentences or notes; completing or labelling diagrams, charts or tables; classifying; matching; choosing paragraph headings and writing short answers.

Exam Tips: As with the listening module, answers are written on an answer sheet, but no extra time is given for this. It is important for learners to practise managing time so that they complete the whole module within the hour by reading quickly and efficiently.

Academic writing

Content: There are two tasks in this module and it lasts one hour. In Task 1, students are expected to describe, compare and contrast information in diagrams, charts or tables using at least 150 words. This might be, for example, a chart showing how young people spend their leisure time. Organization is important and learners need to show that they can clearly present and describe data. Alternatively, students may have to describe the stages of a process, or explain how something works.

In Task 2, an opinion or a problem is stated and students need to write at least 250 words in response to a question related to this. They may be asked to give solutions to the problem, or present arguments in favour and against the opinion, as well as giving and justifying opinions.

Assessment: In Task 1, assessment is based on whether the question has been answered clearly and appropriately, the organization of the text and the accuracy and variety of vocabulary and sentence structure.

In Task 2, assessment uses slightly different criteria and is based on the arguments, ideas and evidence given, as well as the organization of the text and the accuracy and variety of vocabulary and sentence structure.

Exam Tips: Learners are advised to spend 20 minutes on Task 1 and 40 minutes on Task 2. It is important to keep to these timings, as Task 2 is longer, and carries slightly more weight than Task 1. It is also important to keep to the word limits, as writing less than the number of words stated is likely to result in a lower score.

Speaking

Content: The Speaking module takes between 11 and 14 minutes and is an oral interview between the student and an examiner. It will be recorded on audio tape. There are three parts to the module. In the first part, (4–5 minutes) the examiner will ask some general questions about home and family, job or studies, hobbies and so on. In the second part (3–4 minutes), the student is given a card with 3–4 prompt questions about a particular topic. They have one minute to prepare, when they can write notes if they wish, and will then be asked to speak on the topic for 1–2 minutes without any interruption. At the end of this section, the examiner may ask a question. Finally, in the third part (4–5 minutes), the examiner will ask some more questions related to the topic in the second part. In this section, they will be looking for the candidate to give opinions and express reasons.

Assessment: Assessment is based on fluency, the ability to express oneself clearly and naturally without long pauses, the range, variety and accuracy of vocabulary and grammatical structures, and pronunciation.

Exam Tips: It is important that the candidate tries to be as relaxed as possible in the exam. More extended responses to questions rather than just 'yes' or 'no' answers will gain higher grades. Students can prepare for this module, for example, by practising speaking for 1–2 minutes on different topics. However, discourage the memorisation of long speeches as examiners can usually spot this, and will ask learners to talk about something else.

Band 9 – Expert User
Has fully operational command of the language: appropriate, accurate and fluent with complete understanding.

Band 8 – Very Good User
Has fully operational command of the language with only occasional unsystematic inaccuracies and inappropriacies. Misunderstandings may occur in unfamiliar situations. Handles complex detailed argumentation well.

Band 7 – Good User
Has operational command of the language, though with occasional inaccuracies, inappropriacies and misunderstandings in some situations. Generally handles complex language well and understands detailed reasoning.

Band 6 – Competent User
Has generally effective command of the language despite some inaccuracies, inappropriacies and misunderstandings. Can use and understand fairly complex language, particularly in familiar situations.

Band 5 – Modest User
Has partial command of the language, coping with overall meaning in most situations, though is likely to make many mistakes. Should be able to handle basic communication in own field.

Band 4 – Limited User
Basic competence is limited to familiar situations. Has frequent problems in understanding and expression. Is not able to use complex language.

Band 3 – Extremely Limited User
Conveys and understands only general meaning in very familiar situations. Frequent breakdowns in communication can occur.

Band 2 – Intermittent User
No real communication is possible except for the most basic information using isolated words or short formulae in familiar situations and to meet immediate needs. Has great difficulty in understanding spoken and written English.

Band 1 – Non User
Essentially has no ability to use the language beyond possibly a few isolated words.

Band 0 – Did not attempt the test
No assessable information provided.

Further information and strategies on how to approach the IELTS exam are detailed in this book, the Student's Book and the Study Skills Book.

Contents of the Teacher's Book

Contents of the Student's Book

Content overview

Themes

This unit acts as an introduction to the different parts of the IELTS exam and is thematically focused on the experience of studying abroad.

Exam related activities

Reading

Multiple choice

Writing

Task 1 Understanding key features of data
Writing an introductory statement
Describing data which show changes over time

Listening

Part 1 Form filling
Part 2 Table completion
Note completion

Speaking

Part 1 Expanding answers
Part 2 Describing activities and food
Part 3 Discussing aspects of culture shock

Language development

Language focus and Vocabulary

Forming questions
Dependent prepositions
Understanding how sentences work
Quantifiers

Skills development

Reading

Skimming
Prediction
Diagrams

Study skills

Ways of recording vocabulary

Dictionary focus

Listening 1 p6

Why study IELTS?

Exam information
This listening is similar in style to Part 1 of the IELTS Listening module, which is the easiest text of the four in the exam, and is a dialogue on a non-academic topic. The context is often students in a social setting, or as in this listening, a student talking to a university staff member about admissions, housing or other non-academic subjects.

CD#2 **1** 01 Ask students to look at the photo of Li Cha and to speculate about her. Draw their attention to the questions and ensure they understand *contact number*. Then play the recording.

Suggestion
Note that in the IELTS Listening module, all recordings are only heard once. However, at the beginning of this course, students will probably still need the security of hearing recordings twice.

Answers

1 18
2 2B
3 29th October
4 0825 701 6924 (note, the other number is in Hong Kong)
5 (about) 3 (years)

(AO = Admissions Officer; LC = Li Cha)

AO: Hello Li Cha, I'm Susie Shaw, the Admissions Officer.

LC: Hello, pleased to meet you.

AO: I'd just like to talk to you to find out a little more information to give your new tutor, Stephen Ennis.

LC: OK.

AO: How old are you, Li Cha?

LC: I'm eighteen.

AO: OK. Now your start date is next Monday, that's the 14th February. And you're in class 2B.

LC: Sorry, 2D?

AO: No 2B. B for Bravo. Do you know when you're finishing? October or November?

LC: I'd like to go home and see my family in November.

AO: Finishing at the end of October then, the 29th. We need a contact number here and one in China, Li Cha. Do you live with your parents?

LC: No, I live with my grandmother and brother, Shao, in Hong Kong. Their telephone number is 8731 4591. And my mobile number here is 0825 701 6924.

AO: Obviously you've studied English before. How long have you been studying?

LC: About three years.

AO: Is that all? You must work hard! I thought you'd been studying for at least five years. Do you have any other hobbies?

LC: Well, I like playing table tennis. I also spend a lot of time emailing friends. Oh, and I like reading. I read in English sometimes too.

AO: Great, that's probably why your English is so good. Now, you want to take IELTS, don't you? Why's that?

LC: Well, I want to go to the University of Sydney. I'd like to study IT and computing.

AO: Really? Would you like to get a job in IT in the future?

LC: Yes, I'd really like to work with computers, there are just so many possibilities.

Language focus 1 p6

Forming questions

Aim
The language focus sections in this book are designed to improve common areas of difficulty. Sometimes students know the rules, but do not apply them in practice. Therefore, many of the activities employ a 'discovery' type approach, to enable you to assess how much help students need with this area.

1 Go through the table and the first example with the students. Then ask them to write questions for the other answers. Monitor and then correct. Use this opportunity to present question formation including subject / object questions.

Refer students to the Grammar section on page 150.

Answers
1 How old is he?
2 What are your hobbies?
3 Why are you taking IELTS?
4 What are you going to study?
5 What would you like to do in the future?

2 Ask students to work individually to correct the mistakes.

Answers
1 Can you speak Chinese?
2 How often do you speak English?
3 How old are you?
4 Why did you go there?
5 Who is teaching you? / Who teaches you?
6 What are you doing?
7 How do I / you complete this form, please?
8 Where does he live now?
9 When will you go home? / When are you going home?
10 What time does it start?

Speaking skills p7

Expanding answers

Aim
This book aims to develop students' speaking skills with a particular focus on expressing opinions backed up by reasons, and also to help them produce more extended turns. Although activities are primarily in IELTS contexts, the practice given will also help prepare students for seminar and presentation situations at university.

1 This activity should encourage students to give fuller answers in the first part of the Speaking module. Ask students to match the short answers with the possible expansions. Feedback as a whole class and check any vocabulary problems.

Answers
1 b
2 a
3 e
4 g
5 f or d

Speaking 1 p7

Exam information
In Part 1 of the IELTS Speaking module, the examiner will ask general questions related to studies, family, future plans and other familiar topics. It is important that students give full rather than brief or monosyllabic answers.

Aim
This section introduces Part 1 of the IELTS Speaking module. It gives opportunities for students to practise forming questions and to find out about each other.

1 Students write down five questions around the topics given, eg *Where do you come from?* Monitor to check accuracy, referring back to Language focus 1.

Possible questions

1 Where do you live?
2 Have you got any brothers and sisters?
3 Do you have any hobbies?
4 What would you like to study?
5 What would you like to do in the future?

2 Remind and encourage students to produce expanded rather than brief replies. In pairs, students take it in turns to play roles of the examiner and candidate. As part of whole-class feedback, listen to one pair doing the task then ask a few students to report back on the information they found about their partner.

Listening 2 p8

Exam information
This listening text is similar to a Part 2 text in the Listening module. This is a monologue on a non-academic subject, and is slightly more difficult than Part 1. These kind of texts may or may not be in a university context, but they will not be part of a lecture. They will be a talk on a more general subject.

1 02 Lead into this listening by telling the students that Professor Gooding is going to talk about the difficulties she has had in adjusting to living in different countries, and elicit the kind of problems they think she might have had in the countries in the table. Encourage them to predict what kind of words they are listening for.

Exam information
Note that the instructions state no more than three words for each answer. This is a common IELTS instruction. Ensure students understand that one, two or three words are acceptable.

Answers

1 looking different / being tall
2 (the) (extreme) heat
3 Finland
4 read (anything / Japanese)
5 eat with / use chopsticks

extreme = very great or intense (adj.) (also) = maximum, beyond normal limits

02

Hello everyone. Thanks for coming this evening. I've been invited here tonight by the International Students Society to talk a bit about culture shock. For many of you who have recently arrived from your home countries, life here in New Zealand must seem quite strange and different to you in many ways. Because of my work as an anthropologist, I've had the opportunity to work in quite a number of different countries with quite diverse cultures, so I've had my fair share of culture shock and know exactly how you might be feeling at this time.

Tonight, I want to talk a bit about my own experiences of culture shock and then go on to give you a few hints on how to minimize the effects.

I first left New Zealand when I was only 22 to do some research work on the island of Sumatra in Indonesia. I was interested in learning all about the country and the people, but I was particularly fascinated by the architecture.

In the part where I was working, the buildings have beautiful, curved roofs that I had never seen before and I loved them!

Life in Indonesia is very different from life in New Zealand, and at first I found it very difficult to adjust. The worst thing was looking different to everyone else. I'm about average height in New Zealand, but in Indonesia, I was much taller than most people, and it made me feel very uncomfortable. One of the best things, though, was the food. A change in diet can be one of the biggest problems of moving to a new country, but for me Indonesia was not difficult from that point of view. I'm very keen on spicy food, and there is an Indonesian chicken curry called 'Rendang' that is out of this world!

Climate can be another thing that people find it difficult to adjust to. I found working in Egypt very difficult because of the extreme heat. In contrast, living in Finland was hard because during the winter months the days are so short. Where I was, in the North, it was only light for about four or five hours a day in December. By the end I was pretty good at cross country skiing, though!

Language is often one of the biggest barriers when you're settling into a new country, but I'm quite good at learning them and this hasn't usually been a problem for me. However, Japan was quite different. I had learnt some spoken Japanese before I went, but I hadn't tried to learn to write, so initially, I was a bit nervous about going to a country where I couldn't read anything. This did make life a lot more difficult for me. I couldn't read the destinations on buses, or menus in restaurants, or even road signs.

Sometimes it can be very small things that you're not used to that can make you feel the most homesick. For me, in China, it was connected with eating again. I really love Chinese food, but I found it very difficult to eat with chopsticks. I did learn eventually, but I still prefer a fork! One of the best things about my stay in China, though, was the Professor I was working with at the university. He was really enthusiastic about his work, and that made my job very satisfying.

OK, well enough about my experience. Having mentioned some of the problems I faced, I want to look a bit more generally at how you can adapt to culture shock …

Vocabulary p8

Dependent prepositions

1 Look at the example and check students understand the idea of dependent prepositions. Then ask them to find five adjectives with dependent prepositions in the Speaking skills, Expanding answers section on page 7.

Answers

Sentence a: good at, interested in
Sentence c: nervous about
Sentence d: frightened of
Sentence f: fascinated by

> Write on the board

Keen = enthusiastic about
(UK) Keen on spicy food
(USA) Keen about swimming

2 Ask students to complete the sentences from the recording with the correct preposition. Do not correct at this stage.

3 ▭ 02 Students listen again and check their answers in pairs. Then quickly check them as a class.

Answers

1	by	fascinated by
2	from	different from
3	on	keen on
4	at	good at
5	about	nervous about
6	about	enthusiastic about

interested in

4 Looking at sentences 0 and 5 from exercise 2, elicit that we use an -ing form after a preposition.

5 Students add the missing prepositions to the sentences.

Answers

1	in	interested in
2	by	fascinated by
3	from	different from
4	on	keen on
5	about	enthusiastic about
6	about	nervous about

6 Students work in small groups to talk about different countries and cultures. The first person rolls a dice and has to talk about the statement corresponding with the number shown on the dice. Encourage use of adjective / preposition combination.

It is important that you encourage your students to notice and make a note of verb / adjective / noun + preposition combinations as they read or learn new vocabulary. Encourage them to do this with the words in each Dictionary focus, for example.

Reading 1 p9

Aim
This text has been written for students studying in the UK. The level of the language is therefore not as complex as that they may find in the IELTS exam. This enables them to start to develop some of the key skills, such as predicting, skimming, matching text with diagrams and choosing the right option in multiple choice, without struggling too much to comprehend the text.

1 If you think your students may know, you could ask them to define 'culture shock' before they read the text. If not, simply ask them to read the first part of the text and then elicit from them what it means.

2 Ask them to read the first part again to find as many different causes of culture shock as they can.

Answers

- shock of a new environment, meeting lots of new people and learning the ways of a different country
- being separated from the important people in your life: people you would normally talk to at times of uncertainty …
- missing familiar sights, sounds and tastes
- being tired and jet-lagged

3 Ask students ~~to work in groups to discuss~~ what they know about Britain and make predictions about what the author will say about the different points.

4 Ask students to read the text and compare what the author says with their predictions or ideas. Tell them to refer to the glossary if they need help with vocabulary.

5 Essentially this is a matching paragraphs to headings task, as often found in IELTS, but it also gives students practice in another useful IELTS skill – interpreting diagrams. Look at the diagram together with the class and check that they understand that the stages are in sequence and that the dip in the curve represents how positive they are likely to be feeling.

Answers

A 4
B 1
C 5
D 2
E 3

Note that if your students are currently studying abroad, they may well recognize some of these feelings and welcome the opportunity to discuss them.

Multiple choice

6 Many students will be familiar with the concept of multiple choice, but encounter them to underline and look for key words (or similar words) and then find the evidence for their choices (or why they have not chosen an option) in the text.

Answers

1 B (paragraph B: ... *you are still protected by the close memory of your home culture.*)
2 A (paragraph E: *Next you may reject the differences you encounter.*)
3 D (encourage students to look at key words: *returning home, promote, warn*)

7 If your students are still preparing to study abroad, you could use this discussion question to allow them to discuss their plans. If they are currently studying abroad, you could focus the discussion either on what they enjoy about living in this country, or on another country they might like to live in in the future.

 The vocabulary section on page 155 contains an exercise on *-ed* and *-ing* adjectives, including many found in the reading text in this section.

Listening 3 p11

Note completion

Exam information
This is another example of a Part 2 text, which practices another common question type – Note completion. Draw students' attention to the fact that Note completion may involve using words exactly from the listening text, or they may have to change the words or the grammatical form to make the answer fit the word limit.

Suggestion
Give students as much support as possible in the early stages of Note completion questions by asking them to predict the possible grammatical form of the answer, eg if the gap is preceded by an article, then the answer must be a noun, or an adjective + noun combination.

1 03 Ask students to look at the notes and predict the kind of information (including what word class) they will need to listen for.

Answers

1 in touch with / in contact with
2 photo(graph)s
3 your country
4 (other) international students
5 (some) support

 03

... so this afternoon we've been talking a bit about culture shock and your experiences of culture shock so far in adjusting to life in this country. Maybe this hasn't happened to you and you're thinking it won't because you're from Europe, or you've done a lot of travelling before. But it is important to understand that culture shock can hit you whatever culture you come from and however well travelled you are. It's a perfectly normal experience, if a little worrying when it does happen to you.

There are some things you can do, however, to help yourself get through it. First of all, do keep in touch with home. Aki, on student reception, can help you to buy a phone card to make cheaper calls home, and you can always email friends and family from the Resource Centre. If you haven't brought any photos of friends and family, get them to send you some, so you can feel at home.

Make sure you eat well – not just crisps and chocolate! And it's a good idea if you can eat some familiar food. Other students from your country will probably be able to help you find shops which specialize in food from your country. And you need to exercise too – not only for your health. And it's a good way of meeting people.

Make some new friends. Get to know the other international students, whether from your own country or others. They will understand something of what you're feeling and their experience may be able to help you. And, if you can, try to make friends with the local home students. That way you can really learn about this new culture – and they can learn about yours.

Let us help you! You're here at the orientation programme, which is a good start, but we also offer a drop-in centre with a student advisor available daily, and personal counselling. You might not use such a service at home, but remember that you perhaps don't have the same support networks of friends and family here, and these services can provide you with some support. The most important thing is to find someone who will listen uncritically and with understanding, rather than isolating yourself.

You need to remember that culture shock is entirely normal and usually unavoidable. It's not a sign that you've made a mistake or can't manage. In fact, it can be a significant learning experience, making you more aware of aspects of your own culture as well as the new culture. It will give you valuable skills which will be part of the benefit of an international education.

Exam information

> **Exam information**
> This section introduces Parts 2 and 3 of the Speaking module. Part 2 may be the students' first experience of a longer, uninterrupted turn or mini-presentation. In Part 3, full responses to questions on a general topic are expected and many students need considerable skills development to produce appropriate answers.

After reading the Exam information box in the Student's Book, check that students understand the basic format by asking comprehension questions: *How long do you have to prepare? What is the minimum time you need to speak for? Will the examiner speak in this section? How are Parts 2 and 3 linked?*

1 For Part 2 practice, put students in pairs (A and B) and ask them to quickly read their card. Tell them to make brief notes on a piece of paper (these could be in English or their own language) and notify them when the one-minute limit is up. Students take it in turns to give their talks to their partner. Monitor and give a two-minute time limit. Allow students to ask a simple follow-up question to each talk. As whole-class feedback, ask a few students to report back on what their partner's talk was about. This should highlight whether any key points on the card were omitted or if the talk was too short.

> **Exam information**
> In Part 2 of the IELTS Speaking module the candidate will have to speak uninterrupted for 1–2 minutes. Encourage the students to:
> • Use the 1 minute preparation time carefully to think about and make a note of what they are going to say
> • Organize their talk in the order suggested on the card
> • Keep their talk relevant to the topic and questions on the card
> Plenty of practice will ensure they become familiar with this type of task.

2 For Part 3 practice, keep students in the same pairs and ask them to take it in turns to select three questions to ask their partner on the general themes of this unit. Monitor responses for the feedback stage, perhaps emphasizing the importance of aiming to produce fluent, extended answers.

> **Exam information**
> In Part 3, the examiner will ask questions broadly related to the theme in Part 2. It is important that the students listen carefully to the questions and then give a longer answer, providing opinions, reasons and examples.

Understanding key features of data

> **Exam information**
> This section introduces IELTS Writing Task 1. In Task 1, candidates often have to describe or present data shown in a diagram. Describing data is also an area that is vital in many academic subjects.

1 Students look at this typical Task 1 question, but do not spend time checking comprehension as this occurs in exercise 3. However, ask how many words they need to write (*150 words*), who they have to write for (*a university lecturer*). Tell them that in the exam they will have 20 minutes to complete the question.

2 Key vocabulary is introduced which will be useful to describe data. Ask students to read the words in the box before labelling the diagram. Other representations of data could be elicited at this stage, such as pie charts or tables, by drawing simple illustrations on the board.

Answers

a key
b vertical axis
c bar chart
d horizontal axis
e axes
f line graph

3 Point out that it is very important that students first make sure they understand what a diagram shows. Then it is important to select the main ideas, group information and not simply list every single detail shown. Refer students to the task in exercise 1 so they can answer questions 1–6. Check in pairs before feedback as a class to check understanding.

Answers

1 Years from 96/97 to 00/01
2 Thousands of students
3 Subjects studied
4 b) Changes over time
5 Engineering and Technology, and Computer Sciences
6 Probably b) subjects, as students will probably pick out the fact that some subjects increased in popularity, while others declined.

Writing an introductory statement

4 It is common for students to copy the wording of the question in their opening sentence. Encourage students not to simply write down the questions again but rather try to paraphrase the wording or change it in some way, perhaps by giving a comment about the general trends shown. This extract provides a clear model of a possible opening paragraph.

Answers

1   A: what the graph or chart shows but it is not written using exactly the same wording as the question.
2   C: namely subjects which became more popular and those which became less popular – this also summarizes how the writer has chosen to group the information
3   F: (see above)
4   T: after the main ideas have been introduced, more specific details can be added.

Describing data which shows changes over time

5 Students study the chart again and complete the sentences with the correct subject. This will require them to understand the language for describing trends so, depending on the level of your students, pre-teach this using simple diagrams on the board. Alternatively, use the exercise as a way of discovering how much they know, and clarify meaning afterwards.

Answers

1   Biological Sciences
2   Computer Sciences
3   Engineering and Technology, Computer Sciences
4   Physical Sciences
5   Engineering and Technology
6   Medicine and Dentistry

6 Read the example together. Students make the statements in exercise 5 more detailed by using figures from the chart and phrases from the box.

Example answers

- Biological Sciences showed a steady increase over the five-year period, from 80,000 to over 90,000
- and there was a sharp increase in the popularity of Computer Sciences, especially between 99/00 and 00/01 when numbers increased by nearly 30,000.

See Model answer on page 160 of the Student's Book for more examples.

7 Ask students to look back at exercises 2–6 to construct their answer. This is a very controlled task, but it should provide students with a solid base from which they can answer similar questions in the future.

8 A clear model is provided on page 160 for students to compare with their own answer. They can underline any significant differences they find.

Note that there is further practice of phrases such as *a sharp fall* in the Vocabulary section on page 155.

Understanding how sentences work

Exam information
Even at this level students still often struggle with basic sentence structure, especially word order. In order to achieve a higher IELTS score, accuracy in this area is vital as word order in English often helps clarify meaning.

1.1 It is easier to correct syntactical errors if students are aware of the names of basic parts of speech. Ask students to look at the sample sentence and find examples of each part of speech. If they find this difficult, you could give further practice using other sentences from the text.

Answers

1   an adjective: steady, popular
2   a linking word: however, and
3   a noun: Engineering, Technology, drop, popularity, subjects
4   an article: a, the
5   a preposition: to, of, in, with, from, over
6   an adverb: nearly, still, just

1.2 Use this question to check students understand what a 'subject' is.

Answer

Engineering and Technology

2 Look at the examples as a class, then ask students to divide up the sentences. Strictly speaking some of the 'objects' are in fact complements or adverbials but these all function in much the same way in the sentence. If students are monolingual, you may be able to help them see what pattern(s) their language typically uses, and what if anything, they use as a dummy subject. Many languages use a form of *have* for this purpose, for example.

Answers

	Subject	Verb	Object/Complement/ Adverbial
1	Others	dropped	in popularity
2	This	remained	the least popular subject of the five
3	Biological Sciences	showed	a steady increase …
4	There	was	a sharp increase in …
5	There	was	a slight fall …

3 As well as giving practice, this exercise will also provide a model for the following writing task. Elicit the first one as an example and then let students work individually to put the sections of the text in order. You could copy the following answer onto an OHP for ease of correction, or make paper copies.

Answers

(1) More and more college students from the United States are going abroad to study. (2) In 1997 to 1998, 100,000 American students earned college credits abroad. (3) However, recent figures show that while American students are leaving the country to study abroad, thousands of foreign students are coming to study in the US. (4) In 1997 to 1998, there were 500,000 foreign students studying at American colleges and universities, over 10% more than in the previous year.

Writing 2 p15

1 This provides an opportunity to give students practice in a Writing Task 1 activity and to consolidate what has been learnt so far in this unit. Depending on how much support you feel students need and time available, this could be set for homework. Give feedback as appropriate but focus on aspects introduced in this unit.

Answer

See Model answer on page 160 of the Student's Book.

Language focus 3 p16

Quantifiers

Aim
This kind of language is very frequently used in both Task 1 and Task 2 questions (and indeed in all kinds of academic writing). It is also an area where students often make mistakes. Improving their accuracy in talking about quantity (also covered in Unit 2) can make a significant difference to the overall accuracy of their writing.

1 Ask your students to look at the charts and ask questions about which of these sports they enjoy and find out if their likes / dislikes are similar to the ones in the charts. Then ask them to look at the sentences in exercise 1 and ask them to identify mistakes with quantifiers. You could refer them to the box at the bottom of the page if they are not sure what quantifiers are.

Answers

1 The students spend <u>a lot of</u> time watching football. (we prefer not to use much / many in positive statements)
2 <u>The</u> majority of the students prefer watching football to playing it. (majority usually takes the definite article)
3 <u>Some / Some of the</u> students like playing basketball.
4 The students don't spend <u>much / a lot of</u> time playing basketball. (time is uncountable)

5 <u>The</u> number of students who play hockey is larger than <u>the</u> number who play football.
6 <u>A</u> large number of students enjoy watching football.
7 Several of the student<u>s</u> don't play any sport. (a plural group)
8 The students spend <u>a</u> large amount of time watching sport.

2 Many of these rules should have come up in feedback on the previous task. Ask students to choose the best option to complete the rules. Check as a class, using sentences from the previous exercise to illustrate each point.

Answers

1 plural
2 questions / negative sentences, uncountable
3 countable
4 countable, uncountable
5 second

[handwritten: Most / Several / Some + of + noun]

[handwritten: * A number of → countable]
[handwritten: * An amount of → uncountable]

3 Ask students to write more sentences about the information in the bar charts.

For extra practice see the photocopiable activity for this unit on page 114.

Study skills p17

Ways of recording vocabulary

Aim
Lower level learners who are just starting to engage with academic texts often struggle with the more specific academic vocabulary required. Recording new lexis effectively, logically and consistently is crucial. This section aims to show students how to do this.

1 Students write true sentences about themselves.

2 Check that students have drawn appropriate diagrams.

Answers

1 ↗   3 →

2 ↘   4 ↓

3 Students often worry about understanding the definitions in English-English dictionaries. Encourage them to buy one with definitions appropriate to their level.

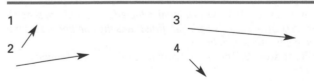

[handwritten: * a lot of → plural noun + plural verb]
[handwritten: * The majority of > plural noun]
[handwritten: The number of]
[handwritten: * Much < questions / negative statements (uncountable nouns)]
[handwritten: * Many → Countable nouns]

Answers

1 a
2 e
3 d
4 f
5 g
6 c
7 b

Finally ask students which methods from the Study skills section they liked best and elicit discussion of the ways students currently record vocabulary.

> **Suggestion**
> Encourage students to keep vocabulary notebooks, using the methods outlined here appropriately. This is also an opportunity to talk about recording pronunciation phonemically, marking word stress, and including information on collocation, dependent prepositions, etc.

Dictionary focus p17

Students should first find the word in context in the unit. They can then check the appropriate part of speech before looking the word up in a dictionary.

In order to encourage good dictionary use, you could ask some questions about such things as countability, word stress and collocations. Some sample questions you could ask are included below.

Eliminate (page 10: *eliminate answers which are clearly wrong.*)
What preposition can be used with *eliminate*?
Eliminate sthg _____ sthg.
What is 'a process of elimination'?
Adjustment (page 10: *stages of adjustment experienced during orientation.*)
Is *adjustment* countable, uncountable or both?
What verb and adjective are part of the same family?

Potential (page 10: *You may feel full of potential and able to trust yourself in all kinds of situations.*)
Reject (page 10: *Next, you may reject the differences you encounter. You may feel angry or frustrated, or hostile to the new culture.*)
Accept (page 10: *Differences and similarities are accepted.*)
Minimize (page 11: *Ways to minimize the effects of culture shock.*)
Illustrate (page 12: *This bar chart illustrates the number of students studying different subjects ...*)
Specific (page 13: *The second sentence tells us about specific subjects.*)
Statistic (page 13: *Do not simply list every statistic.*)

Vocabulary recycling

Vocabulary notebooks

One of the best ways for a learner to gain and retain new vocabulary is to keep a vocabulary notebook. This should be pocket-sized, so that it can be carried around easily, but not so small that it is inconvenient to write in. You could ask all of your students to bring in a cheap notebook to class and give them suggestions on how to use it.

This may include the following sections, or others:
* Words recorded alphabetically (remember that letters such as Q, X, Z, Y, etc, will not require as much space as other letters.
* Subject headings, eg words about crime, etc.
* Grammatical headings, eg phrasal verbs, dependent prepositions
* Skills related headings, eg useful phrases for Part 2 writing questions, words to describe graphs, etc.
* How the book is arranged is very much up to each individual, but try to encourage students to include more information (see Study skills above) than simply bilingual lists.

Content overview

Themes

This unit focuses on overpopulation and some of its effects on the Earth today.

Exam related activities

Reading

Matching paragraphs to headings
Short answers
Choosing the best title

Writing

Task 2 Organizing your writing
        Understanding the question
        Brainstorming and planning
        Drafting and editing

Listening

Part 3 Short answers
        Sentence completion

Speaking

Part 3 Giving and justifying opinions

Language development

Language focus and Vocabulary

Subject-verb agreement
Present simple vs. present continuous
Quantifiers

Skills development

Reading

Prediction
Guessing meaning from context

Pronunciation

Numbers and figures
Sentence stress

Study skills

What makes a good learner?

Dictionary focus

---

1 Look at photos and elicit some different modes of transport onto the board. Then put students into pairs or small groups and ask them to discuss the advantages/disadvantages of these different modes.

Alternatively you could ask students to prepare a short (1–2 minutes) presentation comparing and contrasting two different modes of transport, which they then present to another student.

Reading 1 p18

Prediction

Exam information
The IELTS exam is designed to distinguish between students at very different levels of English. The texts will often be quite complex and contain a lot of unknown vocabulary. However, students should not need to understand everything in order to get a good enough score.

Aim
The exercises with the following reading text encourage students to develop the skills of prediction, looking for key words and scanning, as well as guessing meaning from the context of the text.

1 Ask students to read the first paragraph quickly.

2 Draw students' attention to the key words in bold. Then in pairs, ask them to try and answer the questions.

Answers

1 cars
2 noise, smell, dirt, expense
3 Students' own answers.

Aim

One of the major problems students at this level have with IELTS Reading is that they read too slowly and want to look up every word they don't understand. The aim of this exercise is to encourage them to skim for the information they need, rather than trying to process everything. It may help if they just read the first sentence of each paragraph, usually the topic sentence.

3 Give students a strict time limit to skim the article and check their predictions.

Possible answer

Problems caused by cars.

Guessing meaning from context

Aim

This exercise gives practice in guessing meaning from context and pre-teaches some essential vocabulary for the next reading tasks.

4 Look at the example together. Students find the appropriate paragraph. They should check that the word they have found there could have the same meaning as the definition. Do not allow students to use dictionaries.

Answers

1 EU
2 decade
3 congestion
4 asphyxiated
5 subsidized
6 (on) the Continent

Matching paragraphs to headings

Exam information

Matching paragraphs to headings is a common IELTS task. Again, students do not need to understand or read every part of the text carefully.

5 Show students how key words from the heading are related to words in the correct paragraph. Then ask students to read all the headings first before reading the text again to search for the right paragraphs.

Note that at this early stage of the book there are the same number of headings and paragraphs. This would not usually be the case in the exam.

Suggestion

A useful strategy in the IELTS exam is to highlight or underline the paragraph or section where students found the answer. This is also useful in the feedback slot in order to pinpoint the language used to signify a particular answer.

Answers

1 Paragraph C (*... congestion costs Europe up to £85 billion a year.*)
2 Paragraph D (*... is forecast to increase by 50 per cent ...*)
3 Paragraph F (*Bad policies have increased car and truck use ...*)
4 Paragraph B (*Britons love their cars ... a major new EU study shows.*)
5 Paragraph E (*In Britain that means trying to cut the need to travel,*)
6 Paragraph G (*Brussels wants to cut traffic and pollution with extra taxes ...*)

Short answer questions

6 Again, encourage your students to skim through the text fairly quickly, looking more carefully at sections where they find answers in order to check them. All the answers in this section are numbers or figures to facilitate the development of scanning skills. This would obviously not be the case in the exam.

Answers

1 three times (Paragraph B: *... has tripled ...*)
2 £85 billion (Paragraph C: exact words)
3 50 per cent (Paragraph D: exact words)
4 65 per cent (Paragraph I: exact words)
5 10 per cent (Paragraph I: *... our fares ...* ie Britain's)
6 40 per cent (Paragraph I: *... on the Continent ...* ie Europe)

7 These short answers use words rather than numbers, so are slightly harder to find within the text. Follow the same procedure as above.

Answers

1 cycling and walking
2 lack of investment
3 congestion charging

Choosing the best title

8 Several of the titles are covered within the article, but encourage students to choose the one which best summarizes the whole article.

Answer

5 The solution to road traffic.

Language focus 1 p21

Subject-verb agreement

Suggestion

Subject-verb agreement is another common area of difficulty where it is relatively easy to improve your students' accuracy. Make sure that they understand the countable/uncountable distinction and that we use a singular verb form with uncountable nouns. Also teach them which form goes with common quantifiers, such as *neither of.*

1 Using the sentences extracted from the text, ask students to identify the subject and the verb forms by underlining them. Then get students to decide if the subject is singular or plural. You can then use this information to <u>show how the verb agrees with the</u> <u>subject.</u>

Answers

	subject	verb	singular / plural
1	Bad policies	have increased	plural
2	The cost of alternative forms of transport	is rising	singular
3	Public transport fares	have risen	plural
4	10 per cent of our fares	are subsidized	plural

2 This section focuses on a number of common errors in subject-verb agreement. Students can work together to identify whether the sentences are correct or not and rewrite incorrect ones accordingly.

Answers

0 Nobody <u>seems</u> ... (*nobody* is a singular subject)
1 Correct
2 None of the cars ... <u>were</u> (plural form as *cars*)
3 Correct
4 Most people <u>own</u> a car (*people* takes a verb in the plural)
5 Correct
6 Neither of us <u>travel</u> (*Neither* takes a plural verb form)
7 Correct
8 Car users pay ... (*Car users* takes a verb in the plural)

3 Students should complete the sentences using their own ideas. Monitor to check and elicit a few examples.

 There is extra practice of this area in the Grammar section on <u>page 150.</u>

section on page 150.

Pronunciation 1 p21

Numbers and figures

Aim
Numbers and figures are an integral part of many academic courses as well as the IELTS exam. Students may well understand the figures, but be unable to pronounce them appropriately. This exercise aims to provide practice in a wide range of ways numbers and figures may be expressed.

1 Elicit one or two of the categories from the students (eg *What do we usually measure height in?*) and then ask students to identify what the figures are.

Answers

1 A decimal: 3.75 (NB: three point seven five, NOT seventy five)
2 A date: 13/11/86 (here written with BritEng convention of dd/mm/yy)
3 The size of an area: 600km^2 (NB **square** kilometres OR kilometres **squared)**
4 A height: 6,900m
5 A weight: 30kg
6 A distance: 4,016km (NB thousand, NOT thousands)
7 A price: $450
8 A fraction: ¾(clarify other decimals eg ⅓, and ordinal patterns such as ⅗)
9 A speed: 80 km/h
10 A percentage: 59%
11 A temperature: 54°C
12 A ratio: 4:1

2 You could also ask students to write down examples and ask a partner to pronounce them, or personalize the figures, eg *How tall are you? What proportion of your free time do you spend watching TV?*, etc.

Listening p22

Short answers

Exam information
Although the context of this listening is not strictly academic, it is similar in style to a Part 3 module in the Listening exam. Part 3 is a discussion between up to four people on an academic subject. The context is often students in a seminar or discussing a piece of work.

Ask students how they dispose of their rubbish (including bottles, paper, cans, etc.). Also ask them how they feel if they see people dropping litter and what attitudes people have about this, or what punishments exist for this, in their country.

1 04 Draw students' attention to the Exam information box in the Student's Book. Advise students that 'no more than three words' means one, two or three. Then ask them to underline key words in questions 1–6, and check comprehension of biodegradable and buried before listening.

Answers

1	half a tonne	4	25 million tonnes
2	two-thirds	5	to produce electricity
3	10 per cent	6	2020

(L = Lecturer; J = James)

L: … and today James is going to give us his presentation on household waste disposal. James, are you ready?

J: Yeah, thanks. Well, when I was deciding what to do for this presentation, this topic really attracted me, because it's such an important issue, and it's going to become even more important in the near future when new European law comes into effect. Um … if you have any questions as I go along, please feel free to ask, and I'll do my best to clarify things.
OK. I think the facts and figures speak for themselves: on average we produce 30 million tonnes of solid household waste every year or around half a tonne per person which is a tremendous amount if you think about it, and obviously it's vital that waste is minimized and disposed of in a way that protects our environment and our health.
We're talking about waste food products, packaging, newspapers, glass, garden waste and so on. In fact, some studies have shown that almost two-thirds of our waste is biodegradable; food, paper, natural textiles, for example, and glass makes up about 10%.

L: Sorry, sorry to interrupt, but can I just ask you if those figures are for the UK only, or are the proportions the same in other countries?

J: No, that's fairly universal, at least in the developed world, but different countries do have very different levels of recycling. In Britain for example, we bury in the region of 25 million tonnes of biodegradable waste; this is known as landfill. I'm sure you can imagine that this is a limited option, particularly in a country with a small amount of land. As well as this, 2.5 million tonnes is burned to produce electricity, which is better, but still has environmental problems associated with it, and 2.5 million tonnes is recycled or composted.

L: This is the current situation in the UK?

J: Yes, it is. However, new European law requires us to reduce amounts of waste, and by 2020 we will only be able to send 10 million tonnes of this for landfill and the rest will have to be recycled, burned or treated in a different way. So clearly things are going to have to change, and everyone is involved in this issue in some way …

L: So what exactly is being done?

J: Well, the policy of the government and of environment agencies is firstly to reduce the amount of waste we create to begin with, and secondly, to reuse the waste that is created. Obviously some disposal is necessary but the aim is to limit this as much as possible. What we need to do is to conserve raw materials, like tin and aluminium, while still protecting the environment and public health.

L: Yes, but what does this mean in reality?

J: There are quite a few things that are being done, mostly by local councils. They're responsible for household 'dustbin' collections, or taking away all the rubbish you produce in the home. In recent years, many more sites have been set up to collect waste separately for recycling. There are often containers in car parks or outside supermarkets for people to put bottles in: clear, green and brown bottles are separated. Also newspapers and magazines can be recycled as well as tins made of aluminium. One of the problems of this, though, is that most people are not bothering to take their rubbish there. To overcome this, some local councils also provide special containers, often called 'recycling bins' for residents to collect glass and paper in. They put these outside their houses at the same time as their rubbish, and they are collected and recycled.

L: I see. So are you saying that recycling is more important than actually reducing waste?

J: No. Nowadays, many products are increasingly being designed with reuse or recycling in mind and I think, in general, people are far more aware about these issues. In some countries, like Switzerland for example, they have put a tax on black rubbish bags, so that people are encouraged not to just throw things straight in the bin, and to reduce their rubbish. Having said that, I think it's still absolutely crucial for the government to continue raising peoples' awareness of the importance of waste management and disposal. Overall, the situation has improved over the past 25 years, and this is mainly because of new laws with tighter controls and higher standards. Even so, individuals and businesses still need to work very hard to reduce and reuse waste as much as possible.

L: Thank you very much. That was a very nice presentation. Does anyone have any further questions? …

Sentence completion

2 Give students some time to look at questions 7–14. Encourage them to predict the kind of answers that would fit grammatically before listening again, eg 7 must be a verb in the infinitive form.

> **Suggestion**
> Note that at this early stage we suggest listening twice, looking at half the questions each time. However, you could choose to look at all the questions 1–15 first, and then listen once only, reflecting what would happen in IELTS.

Answers

7 reduce
8 reuse
9 collect dustbins (or waste) / take away rubbish
10 bottles
11 newspapers
12 magazines
13 recycling bins
14 (black) rubbish bags

Language focus 2   p23

Present simple vs. present continuous

Aim
Many languages do not make a distinction between simple and continuous aspect, which can lead to confusion for students. This exercise looks at the two in context, drawing out the major uses.

1 Ask students to underline examples and compare their answers. This should check that students can recognize the two tenses as well as providing examples in context. Make sure that students do not confuse the *-ing* form with present continuous (ie *responsible for … taking away all the rubbish*).

Answers

J: <u>There are quite a few things that are being done</u>, mostly by local councils. <u>They are responsible</u> for household 'dustbin' collections, or <u>taking away</u> all the rubbish <u>you produce in the home</u>. In recent years many more sites have been set up to collect waste separately for recycling. <u>There are often containers in car parks</u> or outside supermarkets for people to put bottles in: <u>clear, green and brown bottles are separated.</u> <u>Also newspapers and magazines can be recycled</u> as well as tins made of aluminium. One of the problems of this, though, is that <u>most people are not bothering</u> to take their rubbish there. To overcome this, <u>some local councils also provide</u> special containers, often called 'recycling bins' for residents to collect glass and paper in. <u>They put these outside their houses</u> at the same time as their rubbish, and <u>they are collected and recycled</u>.

L: I see. <u>So are you saying</u> that recycling is more important than actually reducing waste?

J: No. Nowadays, <u>many products are increasingly being designed</u> with reuse or recycling in mind and <u>I think, in general, people are far more aware about these issues.</u>

2 Students now use the examples they've underlined to illustrate the rules.

Sample Answers

Present simple
1 clear, green and brown bottles are separated / They put these outside their houses … / they are collected and recycled.
2 newspapers and magazines can be recycled / They are responsible / There are often containers in car parks / some local councils also provide / people are far more aware

Present continuous
1 So are you saying …?
2 There are quite a few things that are being done, / many products are increasingly being designed / most people are not bothering to take their rubbish there.

Note:. You could also point out to the students that stative verbs (eg *know, own*) are not commonly used in the continuous forms.

Further practice of this area can be found in the Grammar section on page 150.

Pronunciation 2   p24

Sentence stress

Aim
English is a stress timed language, ie words which carry the key meaning of the utterance are stressed. Usually these are the content words, such as nouns and verbs, eg He LIVES in MANCHESTER. However, we may stress other words in order to make them carry more meaning, eg HE lives in Manchester, or He lives IN Manchester. These exercises aim to make students both more aware of the usual rhythm of English, and how the usual stress can change.

1 Using the example sentences, ask students to underline which words they think would usually be stressed. Do not confirm answers at this stage.

2 🔲 05 Students listen to the recording and check their answers to 1. Then elicit the correct stress patterns onto the board and establish that usually nouns, verbs, and adjectives (content words) are stressed. Pronouns, articles, auxiliaries (function words) are not usually stressed.

Answers

1 keeping <u>animals</u> in <u>zoos</u> is really <u>cruel</u>.
2 they <u>cause</u> so much <u>noise</u> and <u>pollution</u>.
3 I'm <u>convinced</u> that more <u>people</u> would <u>recycle</u> if …

🔲 05

1 If you ask **me**, keeping animals in zoos is **really cruel** because they're taken away from their natural habitats and have far less space than they do in the wild. I **honestly** think that animals should remain in their original environments.

2 I can't **stand** the fact that cars are still allowed in many city centres – they cause so much noise and pollution. I **much** prefer city centres that are pedestrianized, where people can walk around with no worries about too much traffic.

3 I guess I'm quite **lazy** really as I don't bother recycling much except newspapers. I know we should try and reuse our resources if possible, but sometimes it's just not convenient. I'm **convinced** that more people would recycle stuff if there were better facilities, and it was generally easier.

3 Look at the sample sentences and briefly ask students to predict which words are stressed. Based on what they have just learnt, they may suggest the verbs. Do not confirm or deny at this stage.

4 🔊 05 Students listen to the recording again to check their answers to 3. Elicit that function words are stressed in these sentences in order to emphasize meaning. Drill the stress and intonation patterns as necessary.

Answers

1   if you ask <u>me</u> …
2   I <u>much</u> prefer …
3   I <u>honestly</u> think that …

Speaking skills p24

Giving and justifying opinions

> **Aim**
> This section develops students' ability to give and justify opinions on simple topics.

1 🔊 05 As a lead in, write a simple statement on the board, eg *Women are better drivers than men. Smoking should be made illegal*, etc. Ask for responses.

Explain to students that they will hear three people giving opinions on three different topics. They then need to complete the table by noting down what each speaker broadly feels about the topic and the main reasons given. Students briefly compare answers with their partner before general feedback.

Answers

Topic	Opinion	Main reasons
Zoos	Cruel – Animals should remain in wild	Taken away from natural habitats Lack of space
Cars banned in city centres?	Yes – prefers pedestrianized centres	Noise Pollution
Why recycle?	Good to re-use resources More people would do it if easier / more convenient	Speaker doesn't recycle much as lazy and finds it inconvenient

Optional activity

The recording could be played again for students to identify language used to give opinions, eg:

Extract 1: If you ask me…, I honestly think…

Extract 2: I can't stand the fact…, I much prefer…

Extract 3: I'm convinced that…

Remind students about appropriate stress and intonation patterns.

2 Ask students to give opinions to their partner on the different topics. Draw their attention to the phrases in the box and encourage (but don't force) them to use these. Monitor and invite a selection of responses as whole class feedback. Emphasize the importance of giving reasons for each opinion and elicit accordingly.

3 Allow students to discuss this question briefly in pairs before reporting back to the class.

4 Check that students are clear about the vocabulary, then ask them to individually rank the effects of overpopulation, from the most serious (1) to the least serious (6). They could talk about a particular city if they prefer.

5 Students compare their order with a partner. In a feedback stage, encourage clear reasons for their ranking.

Writing p25

Organizing your writing

> **Exam information**
> This section introduces IELTS Writing Task 2 in which the student is expected to write a subjective essay on a general topic supporting any arguments with relevant ideas and examples or evidence. Although students are preparing to write under exam conditions when taking IELTS, the basic stages of writing an essay are relevant to future academic writing tasks.

> **Aim**
> Many essays suffer from a lack of overall coherence. This unit focuses on approaching the task and planning a suitable answer giving practice in organizing, then writing a typical IELTS Task 2 question stage by stage.

1 Allow students about three to four minutes to discuss an appropriate order, giving reasons for their final choice. Provide students with the logical order below but do not go into details as each stage will be addressed specifically.

Suggested answers

1   Read the instructions and question carefully.
2   Analyse the question.
3   Brainstorm ideas.
4   Note down a rough essay plan organized by paragraph headings.
5   Write the essay.
6   Check for errors.

2 It is vital that students read the instructions and question carefully, so ask them to focus only on the main instructions and the general topic in this question.

3 Allow students one minute to answer the four questions on the key requirements for answering the exam question.

Answers

1   Non-specialist audience
2   Problems caused by cars
3   40 minutes
4   250 words

4 Ask students to identify the actual focus of the question by underlining key words and phrases.

Example answers

'... excessive number of cars ... leads to many problems.'
'Individuals and governments ... public transport'
'... tackle ... problems.'

5 Students discuss answers with their partner.

Answers

1   Writing for a non-specialist audience requires students to write in a semi-formal style but not quite as formal as writing for a university lecturer, for example.
2   Yes, eg *There are too many cars on the road and this causes many problems.*
3   More public transport would be a solution to these problems and the government and individuals have a duty to be involved in this.
4   Write an essay agreeing or disagreeing with the statement, ie whether governments and individuals should consider public transport more. The argument needs to be backed up by relevant ideas and evidence.

6 Elicit one problem caused by traffic and then ask for any associated words or phrases and highlight on the board. Then ask for ideas on how and why individuals and governments might cause some of these problems. Finally, focus on how public transport might offer some solutions, highlighting the links.

Note that the vocabulary section on page 155 contains an exercise on common collocations with traffic and road, which may be useful here.

Example answers

| 1 | **Pollution** | Problems: exhaust fumes, gases, harmful
Vocabulary: carbon monoxide, destroy, leaded/unleaded petrol, etc. |
| | **Traffic Congestion** | Problems: traffic jams, delays, heavy traffic
Vocabulary: lateness, gridlock, etc. |
| | **Road safety** | Problems: accidents, speeding, drink-driving
Vocabulary: dangerous, injuries, deaths, etc. |

2   Over-reliance on the car (for unnecessary journeys)
    Poor and limited public transport services
    Expense of public transport
    Lack of car-sharing/pooling
    Poor road safety – dangerous roads/signs/driving
    Environmentally unfriendly fuels, eg leaded petrol
3   Improve and provide more public transport services
    Reduce public transport costs
    Road safety campaigns / improve roads
    More unleaded petrol
    Increase car/road taxes
4   Use public transport more
    Reduce amount of unnecessary journeys
    Share cars to work
    Drive more carefully

7 Ask students to try and make a rough plan based on their notes so far. Explain that by doing this their essay will be more organized as well as giving them a structure to follow, thus making the writing task easier.

Possible plan

Paragraph 1: Introduction – Increase in traffic in general
Paragraph 2: Problems caused by traffic
Paragraph 3: Public transport – individual solutions
Paragraph 4: Public transport – government solutions
Paragraph 5: Summary of opinions – public transport very important

Monitor and encourage students with good examples to share their ideas with the class.

8 Students write the essay based on notes already generated. You could set this as homework, but set a time limit for them to complete the essay. They will have 40 minutes in the exam, but you could allow a little more at this stage.

9 Editing practice is gained by self-correction and/or peer correction. If done as a class writing activity, tell students to spend the last three minutes quickly reading, checking and correcting their own work. Alternatively, ask them to read another student's piece of work and highlight at least two items that need to be corrected. Collect a sample of these items for whole-class correction (but keep the source of errors anonymous).

10 Tell the class to look at a previous student's answer to this question, then allow them a few minutes to discuss it before correcting obvious errors.

Answers

1   The candidate addresses the question reasonably well stating an opinion that an increase in public transport would be a good idea while commenting on the drawbacks of too much private transport.
2   The essay is well organized into paragraphs with a clear introduction and conclusion and there is a logical progression to the argument. It is approximately the right length (259 words).

3 Grammar, vocabulary and spelling need some attention (see answers below) and use of linking words could be improved. See below for samples from text.

1 Grammar – transport is
2 Spelling – considerably
3 Delete word – the or wrong word – a rise in
4 Word form – fewer people using their own cars
5 Subject-verb agreement – are
6 Punctuation – no full stop before because, so no capital letter
7 Add word – but / who
8 Grammar – increase in the use of

Note: Please note that this is a genuine student answer and not all errors were corrected in this text.

Writing: further practice

11 Follow the procedure as outlined in this section. This could be set as homework or done in class under exam conditions. Correction and feedback is optional but should be based on points highlighted in this unit. There is a model answer on page 161 of the Student's Book.

Language focus 3 p28

Quantifiers

> **Aim**
> This is a very common area of difficulty for students at this level, particularly important in the Writing module. This exercise aims to clarify some of the most important distinctions.

1 Ask students to choose from *few*, *a few*, *little*, *a little* to replace the words in italics. Monitor and then look together at the grammar explanation before eliciting answers.

Answers

1 little
2 A few
3 Few
4 a little

2 Students underline the best alternative. As above, ask them to do the exercise before looking at the grammar explanation. This should give you some idea of how big a problem this area is for them. Look at the explanation together and then check answers.

Answers

1 needs
2 Each
3 all
4 all

3 Students complete the gaps with the most suitable option. Follow the procedure as above.

Answers

1 either
2 Neither
3 both
4 Neither

4 Here students again underline the best alternative, before checking with the grammar explanation.

Answers

1 other
2 another
3 other
4 another

Study skills p29

What makes a good learner?

1–3

> **Aim**
> This section is designed to raise students' awareness of the good study habits they have, and others that they could use. Many of these skills will be developed in the Study skills sections throughout the book.

Encourage discussion of these strategies, eliciting and giving advice on how they could be achieved, eg ask them where they make a note of academic words they have learnt, etc. Ask students to fill in the box and review this at a future date, perhaps after two to three weeks, to encourage good habits.

Dictionary focus p29

As in Unit 1, ensure students understand that many of these words can be useful in academic writing, ie for productive use. Ask them to find the words in the context of the unit before looking them up in a dictionary.

major (page 19: ... *a major new EU study shows.*)
force (page 19: *the EU is to consider forcing airlines to pay a tax on aircraft noise.*)
measure (page 19: ... *Britain's weakening resolve to push congestion charging and other green measures.*)
interpretation (page 21: *Academic courses often involve the interpretation and analysis of different numbers and figures.*)
analysis (page 21: *Academic courses often involve the interpretation and analysis of different numbers and figures.*)

category (page 25: *Rank these problems, putting numbers next to the **categories**.*)

evidence (page 26: *Express ideas and opinions backed up by examples and **evidence**.*

urban (page 27: *Overpopulation of **urban** areas has led to numerous problems.*)

individual (page 27: *... and suggest ways that governments and **individuals** tackle these problems.*)

This is also a good opportunity to recycle words from the Dictionary focus in the previous unit.

There are further exercises on some of these words in the photocopiable on page 115.

Vocabulary recycling

Vocabulary box

A useful way to encourage recycling of vocabulary in class is to keep a vocabulary box. This can be anything from an envelope to a biscuit tin, the important thing being that it contains slips of paper or card, each with a single word or phrase written on it. These words could be from the Dictionary focus sections at the end of each unit, and also other vocabulary from the coursebook and from your lessons. You may wish to include a phonemic transcription on the card, or other relevant information, but do not include a definition or translation. Over time, you will quickly build up a stock of vocabulary that has been taught and which can be used in a wide range of recycling activities.

One simple way in which this can be used is as a warmer at the beginning of a lesson. Draw out cards at random from the box, give a definition, and see if students can guess the word. This can be done in teams to introduce an element of competition.

Content overview

Themes

The unit is based around the theme of travel and tourism, and looks at some less common aspects, such as space tourism and ecotourism.

Exam related activities

Reading

T/F/NG
Short answers
Summary completion

Writing

Task 1　Selecting significant information
　　　　Comparing data and describing trends

Listening

Part 2　Multiple choice
　　　　Classification
Part 1　Table completion
　　　　Labelling a diagram

Speaking

Part 2　Giving advice
Part 3　Discussing impact of tourism

Language development

Language focus and Vocabulary

Articles

Skills development

Reading

Skimming and scanning
Guessing meaning from context
Prediction
Reading for gist

Listening

Listening for gist

Study skills

Reflecting on what you have learnt

Dictionary focus

Start by eliciting ideas on what a normal or typical holiday might be. Then look at the photos showing more unusual holidays. Identify what these show with the students and ask if any of them have heard of these before. Then put students in pairs or small groups to discuss the lead-in questions.

Note that there is an exercise focusing on a range of synonyms for *trip* in the Vocabulary section on page 156.

Reading skills　p30

Skimming and scanning

Exam information

Two of the skills practised in this unit are skimming and scanning (looking through a text for some specific piece of information in the way that you might look through a telephone directory.) Both of these skills are necessary in academic life and both are tested in the IELTS exam.

Ask students to look at the headline: *First space tourist grins down on planet Earth.*

Elicit or demonstrate the meaning of the word *grin*. Ask students in pairs to predict the content of the article. Do any of them know about the story?

Aim
This activity is aimed at encouraging students to scan quickly for information, rather than trying to understand every word.

1 Tell the students that they have to find numbers in the text and identify what they refer to. Do the first one as an example, and then do the rest as a race. Students should answer as quickly as they can. Check the answers together.

Answers

1 Dennis Tito's age (line 3)
2 Distance (in miles) of the International Space Station from the Earth. (line 8)
3 Length (in days) of the trip to space (line 8)
4 Cost of the trip in million pounds (line 9)
5 Kilos of luggage allowed (line 30)
6 Number of family members who saw Tito take off. (line 52)

2 Ask your students to look at the three questions in this exercise before they read the text in more detail. Give them five minutes to read silently, without using dictionaries. Reassure them that they do not need to understand everything as they will be given more opportunities to read the text. Although True/False is not an IELTS exercise, students should be familiar with this question type.

Answers

1 True (lines 2–3: *the most expensive holiday in history.*)
2 False (lines 28–29: *to sleep only in Russian sections of the craft.*)
3 False (lines 69–70: *I do miss a good hamburger,*)

Suggestion
It will help to develop your students' comprehension skills to ask them to identify the sections in the article where the answers are located.

Reading 1 p30

True, False or Not Given

Exam information
The exercises in this section more closely reflect the IELTS format.

1 Check that your students understand the concept of 'not given'. Then ask them to read the statements before looking for the information in the text.

Answers

1 TRUE (line 18: *sunny blue skies*)
2 NOT GIVEN (line 28: *we only know that he slept in Russian sections of the craft.*)
3 FALSE (line 38: *Amateurs have flown in space before …*)
4 FALSE (lines 42–47: *The final countdown began at 3am Moscow time, when … were awoken at their hotel.*)
5 NOT GIVEN

Short answers

2 Encourage students to look for key words from the questions in the text. Note that in the IELTS exam the students are more likely to find synonyms than direct repetitions of words from the questions, but at this stage it is useful for them to have this support.

Answers

1 line 49: *doctors washed the crew with a <u>special alcohol lotion</u>*
2 lines 54–55: *Suzanne, <u>his former wife</u>*
3 line 57: *After a <u>40 minute</u> ride to the test centre.*
4 lines 67–68: *soups, juice, tea and coffee, all in <u>toothpaste-like tubes</u>*

Guessing meaning from context

Aim
As students will not be able to use their dictionaries in the exam, it is vital that they develop the skill of guessing meaning from context. This will require plenty of practice.

3 In this exercise, multiple choice answers are given to make the task easier. Students can do the exercise and check answers with their partners. Draw their attention to the part of speech that the word is, as this will help with comprehension, eg if it precedes a noun, it is likely to be an adjective, etc.

Answers

1 C
2 A
3 A
4 B
5 A
6 B

Language focus p32

Articles

Aim
This exercise deals with the basic rules of use for definite and indefinite articles. This is a complex area of English and if your students particularly struggle with this, you might also like to look at the rules for the use of the zero article.

1 Ask the students to match the examples to the rules. Go through the answers with the class, showing how in some cases, the wrong answer can change the meaning, eg Andrea Bocelli, a blind tenor (which implies that he is not very famous, or that there are many blind singers in Italy).

Answers

Indefinite articles
1 c
2 b
3 a

Definite articles
1 c
2 b
3 d
4 a

2 Students complete the gaps and then check against the text. For further practice, you can create exercises like this with other texts they read. There is a summary of rules and further practice in the Grammar section on pages 150–1.

Answers

1 a, the
2 a
3 The
4 A
5 a
6 The, the
7 A, a
8 the
9 the
10 a

Listening 1 p33

Listening for gist

Lead in by asking students about school or college trips they have been on.

1 06 At this early stage in the course, students will still probably need to hear the listening texts more than once. Look at the questions, play the recording and then compare and check answers.

Answers

1 Paris
2 five days

 06

Hello. Can I just have your attention for a minute? Thank you. My name is Mary Golding, some of you may recognize me – I used to be a teacher here at the college, but I changed jobs last year, and I <u>now work as the Student Officer</u>. OK, well, I'm in today to tell you about <u>a trip that we've got going to er … Paris</u>. Well, this'll be a good chance for those of you who haven't been to France before to have a look at another country, and Paris is very beautiful. I think those of you who come will thoroughly enjoy it. <u>The trip is going to be for five days</u>, from the <u>31st March, which is a Saturday</u>, to the 4th April, the following Wednesday. We'll be leaving pretty early in the morning, seven o'clock, from college, so you'll have to set your alarm clocks, and <u>we'll be going through the Channel Tunnel on the train</u>, so no ferries or coaches for those people who get seasick or travel sick! We'll be back again on Wednesday <u>about ten o'clock at night</u>.

Multiple choice

Exam information
Students need to be aware that listening texts often contain distracters – information deliberately designed to catch out students who have not fully understood.

2 06 Tell students to look at all the options first and check any vocabulary, such as *ferry, hovercraft*. Then play the first part of the recording again for students to complete multiple choice answers. After listening, encourage students to check in pairs, discussing why they chose the answers they did, and if they heard any distracting information which would make them eliminate certain answers.

Answers

1 C (possible distraction that she *used to* be a teacher)
2 B (possible distraction that Saturday is not mentioned first)
3 D (possible distraction 'no ferries or coaches.')
4 C (possible distraction 10:00 as the question gives 24 hour clock times)

Classification
3 07

Exam information
Classification tasks are used in both Listening and Reading tasks. Note that, unlike matching tasks, each option can be used more than once or not at all.

Check students understand that they have to use the letters F, I or P, and what they stand for.

Answers

5 I 6 F 7 P 8 I

07

So, what will we be doing when we get there? If you look at the diagram of Paris that I've given you, you can see that we're going to be staying in a small hotel near the centre of town. It's actually in the area called Montmartre. The accommodation will be shared, so you'll be in a room with one of your friends – you can obviously choose who you'd like to share with. On the first day we're in Paris, we'll be going on a boat trip, up the River Seine and up the Eiffel Tower, the famous monument in the middle of Paris. There should be a good view from up there. Both of these things are included in the cost of the trip, so you won't need to worry about spending extra money. On the second day, we'll be going to Notre Dame, which is a large cathedral with beautiful stained glass windows. There's no admission charge for this, but there are lots of souvenir shops around, so you might need some money for those! There will be lots of time for having a look around on your own, and doing some shopping – I know that some of you are very keen on that!

On the third day, our last day in Paris, you'll be free to do whatever you like. You could go to an art gallery, for example the Louvre is a very famous one, where you can see the 'Mona Lisa'. You'll have to pay to get in there, but it's not expensive. The biggest problem is that the queue to get in is often very long. The cost of the whole trip is a hundred and twenty pounds, which includes all of the transport, the hotel, and breakfasts. You'll have to buy other food yourself, so you'll need more money for that. It's a really popular trip, we've had real success with it before, I'm sure those of you who come will really enjoy it.

If you'd like to go, can you sign up on this form on the student noticeboard by Friday. It'll be first come, first served, so do try and sign up as quickly as you can. Thank you very much, I hope to see some of you on the trip.

Reading 2   p34

Prediction

> **Aim**
> Tourism and the environment are both popular topics in the IELTS exam. This text provides some useful vocabulary and ideas.

1 Ask students if they think tourism is always a good thing for a country. You may be able to think of a specific example which will mean something to your particular group of students. Then allow students to brainstorm further ideas in groups.

2 See if students understand the meaning of *ecotourism* and look together at the definition. Elicit ideas about what a good ecotourist should or shouldn't do.

Reading for gist

3 Ask students to read the text quickly to answer the question.

Answer

D All of the above

Guessing meaning from context

4 As well as being an exercise in guessing meaning from context, these verbs are all frequent in academic texts and useful to learn in their own right. Encourage students to use the context rather than their dictionaries to match the definitions.

Answers

1   respect (Point 2)
2   familiarize (Point 10)
3   appreciate (Point 3)
4   exploit (Point 8)
5   encourage (Point 14)
6   introduce (Point 5)

Summary completion

> **Exam information**
> Summary tasks require the students to understand the text in more detail. Some summary tasks in the IELTS exam require the students to use words from the text, some from a box.

5 Ask students to read through the summary and elicit what kind of words they are looking for. Then ask them to read through the text to find words which make sense and work grammatically. Encourage them to underline the section in the text which helped them find the answer. Check in pairs and then whole class.

Answers

1   an ecotour operator (Paragraph 1)
2   local (Paragraph 4)
3   positive (Paragraphs 3 and 5)
4   guests (Point 1)
5   respect (Point 2)
6   soap (Point 11)
7   endangered (Point 14)

Speaking   p35

> **Aim**
> Although the first part of this section is not directly related to the IELTS exam, it provides useful practice in the speaking skills of paraphrasing and expanding answers.

1 Put students in pairs (A and B) and explain that they need to paraphrase their set of guidelines from Reading 2. Encourage students to note down key points and draw attention to the Useful language box: giving advice. Allow preparation time and give assistance before they report back. It may be useful to demonstrate this activity by providing them with one of the guidelines you have paraphrased and elicit from students which words you've replaced.

2 Students work in pairs to ask and answer typical Part 3 questions on this theme. These questions lend themselves quite well to listing answers in note form, so this could be done either as a preparation activity to build confidence or as a follow-up activity led by the teacher. It could then develop into a whole-class discussion.

Listening 2 p36

Prediction

> **Suggestion**
> This is a Part 1 Listening, which introduces the tasks of table completion and labelling a diagram. Ensure students check the format of the table and the order of the questions before listening. Note that the order of the questions always follows the text.

1 Lead in by asking about train journeys and what kind of information it is necessary to know when enquiring about travelling. In pairs or small groups, brainstorm possible questions.

Example questions

1   1 What time does the train leave for Edinburgh?
    2 Do I have to change trains?
    3 What time does the train get to/arrive at Edinburgh?

2   1 Which station are you travelling from?
    2 When would you like to travel?
    3 What time of day would you like to travel?

Table completion

2 Before listening to the recording, draw the students' attention to the strategy and tip boxes on page 36, and encourage them to predict the kind of information they will be listening for.

Answers

Date: 1
Type of ticket: 2 and 3
Times: 4 and 5
Change or direct: 6

3 08 Students listen and complete the table. Allow time for them to check in pairs while you monitor.

Answers

1 (Friday) March 4th
2 Return
3 Standard
4 12.38
5 9.15
6 change at Manchester Piccadilly

08

[TEP = Tele-enquiry person; S = Student]

TEP: Hello, National Train enquiry line. Can I help you?

S: Yes, please. I'd like to find out about times and prices of trains to Edinburgh.

TEP: Fine. And which station will you be travelling from?

S: Birmingham.

TEP: And when would you like to travel?

S: Umm. Friday March the 4th.

TEP: Will that be a Single or Return?

S: Return please.

TEP: Standard or First class?

S: Standard.

TEP: And what time of day would you like to travel?

S: In the morning, please, um, round about 8.00.

TEP: Right, well, there's a train which leaves Birmingham New Street at 8.05 arriving in Edinburgh at 12.38.

S: OK, let me write that down … leaving at five past eight and getting there at … what time?

TEP: 12.38.

S: 12.38. Thanks. Do I have to change trains?

TEP: No, it's direct.

S: And what about the one after that?

TEP: The next one is at 9.15, arriving Edinburgh at 14.35, with a change at Stockport.

S: OK, leaving 9.50, arriving 2.35.

TEP: No, 9.15.

S: Oh. OK. And what about coming back?

TEP: What time would you like to leave?

S: Late afternoon, please.

TEP: Right. There's one at 16.45 which is direct and gets to Birmingham at 20.21, and the one after that leaves at 18.05 arriving at 21.57 including a change at Manchester.

S: Oh, would that be Manchester Oxford Road?

TEP: Erm, no it's Manchester Piccadilly.

4 09 Follow the same procedure as in exercise 3. Students listen to the next part of the recording to complete the table. They should then check their answers together as you monitor.

Answers

7 £33.50
8 7 days
9 Standard Saver
10 No

 09

[TEP = Tele-enquiry person; S = Student]

S: Right. And how much is the cheapest ticket?

TEP: Well, it depends. If you can leave after 9am, it's cheaper. There's an Apex Super Saver which you have to book at least 14 days before you want to travel. <u>That costs £33.50.</u>

S: Thirty three … ?

TEP: Fifty.

S: OK. And what happens if I want to leave before 9am?

TEP: <u>If you can book seven days in advance,</u> then you can buy an Apex Peak Saver. That costs £41.30, but if you can't do that, the next cheapest ticket <u>is the Standard Saver</u> which costs £54 return.

S: So it's £41.30 if I book seven days in advance.

TEP: Yes.

S: And £45 if I don't.

TEP: No, it's £54 for the Standard Saver.

S: Oh, OK.

TEP: If you can travel on a different day of the week, then we have the Off Peak Saver at £38.

S: <u>But I can't travel on a Friday for that fare?</u>

TEP: That's right.

S: Fine. Thanks very much for your help.

TEP: You're welcome.

S: Bye.

TEP: Bye.

Labelling a diagram

Exam information
Labelling a diagram. The kind of diagrams that might be found in IELTS exam questions like this are maps, plans (such as this example), a process or a picture of an object to label.

5 10

Suggestion
When doing this kind of question, it is important that students verbalize, even silently in their heads, the information in the diagram. You can also help them by exposing them to different types of diagrams and encouraging them to describe them to each other, or carrying out describe and draw, information gap exercises.

Give students time before listening to describe the picture of the train station in pairs, including the relative positions of the numbered question boxes. Ensure they notice where the speaker is standing.

Answers

11 ticket office
12 platform 15
13 flower shop
14 toilets

 10

[IDP = Information desk person; S = Student]

IDP: Hello, can I help you?

S: Yes, I hope so. I've just come here by bus, and I'm trying to find my way around the train station. Can you tell me where the ticket office is?

IDP: Yes, of course. Look over there, to your right, <u>the ticket office is to the right of the cafe as you look at it.</u>

S: Oh yes. Thanks. And are those the platforms straight ahead of us?

IDP: Mmm – which one do you need?

S: I think I need platform 15.

IDP: Yes – <u>platform 15 is in the far corner.</u>

S: <u>Sorry, I can't see it …</u>

IDP: <u>Just there, behind the flower shop.</u>

S: Oh yes. Great – just one more thing – can you tell me where the toilets are?

IDP: Sure – <u>they're over there, on the left, behind the newsagent's.</u>

S: Thanks for all your help.

IDP: No problem.

Aim
Some students tend to want to write about every single feature when describing data which often results in a repetitive, inappropriate answer. This section focuses on the skill of selecting significant information and aims to develop students' ability to describe overall trends and changes over a period of time. Language for comparing and contrasting data is also provided.

1 This lead-in activity introduces the topic of tourism in Australia. In small groups, students discuss the questions. You could ask them to estimate how many visitors they think go to Australia from their country (and from the UK).

2 Students read the Task 1 question before discussing their predictions from 1. Ask a couple more questions to check comprehension, eg *How many tourists from Canada visited in 1993?* (48,000), *Which country had most visitors to Australia in 1999?* (the UK).

Task 1: Selecting significant information

3 Students select the most suitable *general* description of the data. It is important that students identify the overall trend from the data quickly. This can then possibly be used in the introductory statement (see unit 1).

Answers

2   There was an increase in the number of visitors to Australia in the 1990s.

4 Students choose three suitable examples of *specific* information. It is important that students are discouraged from writing about all the data in detail and learn to include only key information.

Answers

2   (The *highest* figures for an individual country over the period)
4   (The *biggest overall increase* over the period)
5   (A *significant increase* for an individual country over the period)

The other statements were not as suitable for the following reasons:
1   (not a significant figure in terms of all the data)
3   (statement is inaccurate – figures *decreased*)
6   (not a significant increase in terms of all the data)

5 Students read the model answer and underline specific sentences about each of the countries. Point out or elicit that specific figures are not always mentioned and that descriptions of general trends are acceptable (*Visitors from the United States also increased over the*

decade). Ask for general comments about the sample answer.

Task 1: Comparing data and describing trends

6 This section uses the model to help the students 'notice' key phrases to describe trends or compare data. Establish that the table covers a period of 10 years, so they will need to describe the changes over time. Check understanding of 'trend' and ask students to decide if the phrases in bold refer to trends or comparisons of data.

Answers

Describing trends

(1)   ... increased significantly over the decade.
(3)   ... more than doubled over the period.
(5)   ... which rose from ... to ...
(6)   ... increased over the decade ...
(8)   ... rose over the same period from ... to ...

Comparing data

(2)   The biggest increase was in ...
(4)   The largest number of visitors in total came from ...
(7)   There were considerably fewer visitors ...
(9)   There were almost as many visitors from the United Kingdom as from ...
(10) ... there were nearly as many tourists from other European countries as from ...

Focus on the phrases in the *describing trends* column and the Useful language box. Check understanding of the verbs and adverbs. Use gestures or simple diagrams to clarify.

7 Students read the example before writing a sentence to describe each set of figures.

Answers

1   The number of visitors from the UK rose sharply/significantly between 1995 and 1999.
2   The number of visitors from Canada dropped slightly from 1991 to 1993.
3   The number of visitors from Germany increased steadily from 1991 to 1995.

8 Now focus on the phrases in the Useful language boxes on pages 39 and 40. The students should be familiar with simple comparative and superlative structures but make sure that they know the difference in meaning. Students read the example before writing a sentence to describe each set of figures.

Answers

1 In 1999 there were more than three times as many visitors from the UK as from Germany.
2 In 1991 there were almost / nearly as many visitors from the UK as from the US.
3 The largest / most significant number of visitors in 1999 was from the UK.

Strategy: Writing Task 1

Ask students to look at the statements in the Strategy box and discuss in pairs or small groups which five they think give good advice. Feedback as a class. Discuss why the other sentences do not give appropriate advice.

Answers

1 Describe the data and give examples.
3 Write an introductory sentence saying what the data is describing.
4 Check your grammar and spelling.
6 Start with any general statements and move to specific information.
10 Organize and present the data logically.

Study skills p41

Reflecting on what you have learnt

> **Suggestion**
> Get students into the habit of reviewing the work that they have done, in order to recycle vocabulary and structures, and to clarify anything which has not been properly understood. Try to devote some time to this each week.

1 Ask students to look back over the unit and choose three things they have learnt. They should then put them in order of importance. Obviously, this is a very subjective task, but it should give you some idea of what the students have gained from the unit.

2 In pairs, students discuss why they have chosen these things and how they will be useful. Monitor as they do this.

3 Now ask the students to look back through the unit in more detail to find the answers to the questions. Feedback as a class.

Answers for 3

1 to go up / to rise (page 32)
2 a, (singular countable noun mentioned for the first time) the (unique singular countable noun) (page 32)
3 Look at the parts of the table that are already complete. These will help you to predict the type of answer that is needed. (p36)
4 It is important to … you ought to … (page 35)
5 Make sure your answer is grammatically correct and agrees with what is said in the text. (page 35)

6 dropped significantly/dramatically and rose gradually (page 39). Note that these are not exact synonyms.

4 This question is designed to develop a more reflective approach. You could ask students to discuss in pairs, if you feel this is appropriate, or you could elicit a few examples of how students could get help with things they find difficult (grammar reference books, tutorials, asking a peer for help, and so on).

5 Again, this could be used for pair work discussion, or you could ask students how often they review work, and elicit or make some suggestions.

Dictionary focus p41

As in previous units, ask the students to find the words in context before looking them up in a learner's dictionary for more information.

sustain (page 31: *Tito will be **sustained** by Russian soups, juice, tea and coffee*)
unique (page 32: *Use 'the' with nouns that are **unique**.*)
implication (page 34: *Consider the **implications** of buying plant and animal products.*)
conserve (page 34: *Ecotourism is responsible travel to natural areas that **conserves** the environment.*)
benefit (page 34: *Is there an economic **benefit** going back to or staying in the local community?*)
basic (page 35: *… to expand on the **basic** information.*)
occur (page 39: *… with most of the increase **occurring** in the second half of the decade.*)
contrast (page 39: *This will usually mean comparing and **contrasting** different parts of the information or data.*)
trend (page 39: *Comparing data and describing **trends**.*)

Vocabulary recycling

Backs to the board

Divide the class up into two or three teams. Put a chair for each team in front of the board facing the class. Choose one person from each team to sit in the 'hot seat' and write up one word or phrase that the class have recently learnt on the board. The rest of the team must try to explain or define the word or phrase to the person in the 'hot seat', but without using the word(s) on the board. The person who guesses the word first wins a point for their team. Then change the people in the hot seats for different team members and write up another word on the board.

Although it causes some disturbance, have a different team mate up for each round, otherwise there is too much pressure on the person always in the 'hot seat'.

Content overview

Themes

This unit explores the theme of intelligence, looking in particular at animal intelligence and the idea of multiple intelligences.

Exam related activities

Reading

Table completion
Note completion

Writing

Task 2   Organization and coherence: paragraphing
Introductions
The main body
Conclusions

Listening
Part 4   Summary completion
Multiple choice with more than one option

Language development

Language focus and Vocabulary

-*ing* form and infinitive
Lexical links

Skills development

Listening

Listening and writing simultaneously

Pronunciation

Connected speech

Study skills

Using a dictionary

Dictionary focus

1   Ask students to discuss the question without looking at exercise 2. They will probably find that they have different preferences.

2   Look together at the learning styles associated with their preferences. Students briefly discuss if they feel this is true for them, and the idea that different people learn different ways.

Listening p42

Summary completion

This is the first time in the book that the students have been exposed to a Part 4 Listening, ie a monologue on an academic subject (a lecture). This is the most challenging part of the Listening module.

Exam information
Summary completion is a similar task to sentence completion, with a summarizing paragraph rather than unconnected sentences. Note that answers must be grammatically correct, and, as with all IELTS Listening tasks, correctly spelt.

Aim
In this exercise, students may have to change the form of what they hear in order for it to grammatically fit the summary. In the Listening module itself, they may not have to change the form of the words they hear, but the skill of transforming words is useful, since it trains them to use a different form to answer the question in their own words.

1   🔊 11

Draw students' attention to the strategy box. Look at the tip box together and give them some time to read the first summary and to predict the kind of answers required (including word class). Remind them that they may have to change the form of what they hear in order for it to grammatically fit the summary.

Ask them to underline key words to listen for, eg linguistic intelligence, journalists, teachers, etc. However, make students aware that they may hear a paraphrase rather than the exact word found in the question.

Answers

1 learn languages
2 persuade
3 lawyers

 11

(A = Announcer; JG = John Gregory)

A: As part of our series of study skills talks, John Gregory is going to talk to you today about the theory of multiple intelligences, a way of discovering more about how you, as an individual, may learn best.

JG: Hello. I'd like to start off today by giving you a little background information on the theory and then look at what these multiple intelligences are and how you can learn to make the most of your strengths in different areas.
The traditional view of intelligence, as measured by IQ tests, tends to focus on just two sorts of intelligence – Linguistic and Logical Mathematical, or in other words being good with words or with numbers and logic. In his book, *Frames of Mind*, Howard Gardner suggested that there were in fact other ways of being intelligent, that were not always recognized by the school system. He suggested seven different intelligences, which we will look at today, though he has since increased the number to eight, and thinks there may be more still.
So, what are the types of multiple intelligence? Firstly, those already mentioned. Linguistic and Logical Mathematical. People with linguistic or verbal intelligence are good at communicating with others through words. They will learn languages easily and enjoy writing and speaking. They tend to think in words rather than in pictures. They will be good at explaining and teaching and persuading others to their point of view. Not surprisingly, they will often become journalists, teachers, lawyers, politicians and writers.

2 12 Give them time to read the rest of the summaries, which are longer than would be normal in an IELTS exam, before they listen and complete the summaries.

Answers

4 (make) connections
5 engineering
6 communication
7 recognizing
8 sense of direction
9 play an instrument

12

Those who are strong in Logical Mathematical intelligence are good at seeing patterns and making connections between pieces of information. They reason well, can solve problems effectively. They're the kind of student that asks a lot of questions! They make good scientists, engineers, computer programmers, accountants or mathematicians.

Then there are the Personal Intelligences – Interpersonal, meaning between people, and Intrapersonal, meaning within yourself. Those of you with good Interpersonal intelligence have the ability to see things from other people's points of view, understanding how others feel and think. You encourage people to co-operate and communicate well with others, both verbally and non-verbally. You'll make good counsellors, salespeople, politicians and managers.

Intrapersonal intelligence is more about being able to understand yourself, recognize your own strengths and weaknesses, and your inner feelings. If you're strong in this area you'll make good researchers, theorists and philosophers.

If you tend to think in pictures rather than words, you may be strong in Visual-Spatial intelligence. You enjoy drawing and designing as well as reading and writing. If you tend to doodle on your notes in class, that may be a sign of this intelligence. You'll have a good sense of direction and find graphs, charts and maps easy to understand. A good job for you might be a designer, an architect, a mechanic or engineer.

Bodily-Kinaesthetic intelligence is about the ability to control body movements and handle objects skilfully. Athletes, dancers, actors will be strong in this area. Sometimes physical skills are seen as something entirely separate from intelligence, something which Gardner strongly challenges by including this intelligence.

Finally, Musical intelligence. If you have a good deal of musical intelligence, you'll often play an instrument, but not necessarily. If you often find yourself tapping out rhythms in class, this may be a sign that you're learning through your Musical intelligence. Not surprisingly you'll make a good musician or songwriter.

Multiple choice with more than one option

Exam information
In these questions more than one option has to be selected. How many options are correct is variable. Usually, as in this case, each correct option chosen is worth one mark. Sometimes, usually if the question is easier, all options may have to be correct to gain one mark. In either case it is not important which is written down first.

3 13 Ask the students to look through the options and make sure that they know that they need to choose two activities in each case. They may be able to make some guesses, which they should confirm or disprove by listening.

Answers

10 and 11	B, C
12 and 13	A, D
14 and 15	B, D

 13

If you're aware of where your strengths lie, you can use this information to help you study more effectively. For example, if you have high Linguistic intelligence you'll learn well <u>through group discussions</u>, listening to lectures and <u>reading</u>, whereas if you're stronger in Logical Mathematical intelligence you may learn better through problem solving activities. Those of you with strong Visual-Spatial intelligence will respond well to <u>videos</u>, diagrams and charts. You'll probably find it helpful to learn vocabulary through <u>using mind maps</u>.

If you are interpersonally intelligent, try working in groups or pairs or teaching someone else what you're trying to learn. Your good communication skills mean that you'll also learn well through listening to others. Or, if you're more intrapersonally intelligent, it may be better for you to do some studying alone, setting yourself goals.

If you have high Bodily-Kinaesthetic intelligence you may find it easy to study while walking around – though perhaps you shouldn't try this in class! The Musically intelligent may <u>learn well through songs</u>, or with <u>background music on while they study</u>.

It is important to recognize that everyone is a combination of all the intelligences, just in different strengths. For many tasks and jobs you need to use a combination of strengths. So, what does the questionnaire you've completed tell you about how you learn? ...

Language focus p44

-*ing* form and infinitive

> **Suggestion**
> While this activity will make your students more aware of certain tendencies in terms of which verbs are followed by -ing or infinitive, it is important that you encourage them to use their dictionaries to check verb patterns, and that they should include this information when recording new verbs they learn.

1 Check understanding by asking students to discuss together which 'intelligence' they think they represent.

Answers

0	Bodily Kinaethetic intelligence
1	Visual-Spatial intelligence
2	Interpersonal intelligence
3	Intrapersonal intelligence
4	Logical Mathematical intelligence
5	Musical intelligence
6	Linguistic intelligence

2 Ask students to try and complete the sentences using either an infinitive or an -*ing* form. Clarify any problems in feedback.

Answers

1	visiting (or possibly to visit – AmE)
2	working
3	spending
4	to understand
5	learning / to learn (depends if it's seen as pleasurable in itself or a good idea perhaps in order to learn English)
6	to speak

> **Aim**
> Completing the table will give students a record and enable them to start to see patterns – such as that verbs connected with likes / dislikes often take -*ing*.

3 Ask students to put the verbs from the examples into the table.

Answers

Followed by -*ing*
appreciate
Followed by infinitive
need
would like
Followed by both -*ing* and infinitive
love
like
dislike

Note that although all these verbs can be followed by both forms, the infinitive is mostly used in American English.

4 Use this question to try to elicit from students that we use an -*ing* form after a preposition. This was previously covered in Unit 1.

Answer

Followed by -*ing*

5 Now ask students to categorize the verbs. Encourage them to use their dictionaries if necessary, as this is a good strategy for them to use outside the classroom. You may find it helpful to point out certain patterns or tendencies, such as verbs which convey intentions or desires (*want, decide, plan, hope, wish*) take the infinitive.

Answers

Followed by -*ing*	Followed by infinitive	Followed by both -*ing* and infinitive
avoid consider imagine mind practise involve	agree decide fail hope promise refuse want wish	try begin stop remember forget

6 In pairs, allow students to work through the questions in order to clarify the differences in meaning. Then check answers as a class and provide any further clarification.

Answers

1 a – *like watching* is about enjoyment, in British English
2 b – *like to learn* suggests it is a good idea but not necessarily possible. (eg *I like to wash my hair every day*)
3 c – *Try to do* suggests effort or difficulty. (eg *I tried to stop her, but she wouldn't listen.*)
4 d – *Try doing* is more of a suggestion or an experiment. (eg *I'll try phoning him, he might be in.*)
5 e – If you stop to do something, that is why you have stopped.
6 f – If you stop doing something, you cease that activity.
7 g – *I remember telling him* means that I now have a memory of that event.
8 h – *I remembered to tell him* – the remembering is before the telling.

7 Students work individually to choose the most appropriate form. Check in pairs then as a class.

Answers

1 taking
2 organizing
3 to learn

4 to think
5 setting (or possibly *to set* if there is an idea of difficulty in this)
6 to do
7 to finish
8 starting
9 making

Note that further practice in this area is provided in the Grammar section on page 151.

Pronunciation p45

Connected speech

1 📼 14

Aim
When native speakers speak English, the flow of connected speech causes them to join words together, which can affect the sounds as they join. Sometimes sounds are dropped, or elided. For example, in the phrase *dinner and dancing* the final 'd' of *and* is not pronounced because it slides into the first 'd' of dancing. Another form of elision is called assimilation, where the final sound of a word actually changes in order to facilitate it joining the next word. For example, *Ten people* is usually pronounced as 'Tem people' because 'm' is closer in terms of the shape of the mouth to 'p'. Elision and assimilation can cause difficulties in comprehension for learners who are expecting to hear language pronounced as it is written. It is important for them to be made aware of this to help them comprehend spoken language. It may also help to improve their own pronunciation.

1 Use the 'dinner and dancing' example to establish that the /d/ sound in *and* is elided because it flows into the next sound. Then ask them to look at the next two examples and elicit the missing letters.

Answers

The 't' in *next week* and the 'd' in *brand new* are elided.

Note that 'd' and 't' are often elided before a word which begins with a consonant. Ask them to try saying these phrases with and without the missing letter. It should be easier to say in the elided form, but you may find that your students have difficulty in noticing this difference.

Students then look at the tapescript for recording 14 on page 169 and see if they can find further examples of elision. Remind them to look for places where consonants end and start words. At this stage they will probably also identify places where the sounds are in fact assimilated. As you listen to the recording to check for the answers, you could point the difference out

Answers

The letters in bold in the tapescript show examples of elision.

14

Good morning everyone. We'll start the lecture in a moment, but first I have a few notices. The trip to the City Museum and Art Gallery in Bristol tomorrow has had to be postponed. Mr Struthers is in bed with the flu and no one else is able to take it. I'm told he should be back soon though – if not tomorrow, then the next day, so you should talk to him about the new date. So that's the first thing, the second, is next week is of course the Christmas ball. The venue we're using is brand new and I've been reliably informed that in addition to the usual dinner and dancing, there'll also be ten-pin bowling. There will, however, be a charge of nine pounds for this per team, so why don't you get together with some friends to split the cost. Plus, don't forget it's fancy dress. I expect to see some marvellous costumes! I myself am currently creating something that'll be even better than my Tin Man from the Wizard of Oz of last year.

2 14 Next, using the example 'in Bristol' show how the /n/ sound changes to /m/ before /b/. Students look at the next two examples. Elicit from them what sound changes might be made in them.

Answers

'Tin man' becomes 'tim man'
'Ten pin bowling' becomes 'tem pim bowling'

Note that 'n' will often change to 'm' if it precedes the sounds / m/, /p/ or /b/. This is because the sounds it is changing to are all bi-labial, like /m/. Again, you could ask them to try saying these phrases with and without the changed letter.

Now ask them to look again at tapescript 14 and find examples of assimilation. Start by asking them to find sounds that change before /m/, /p/ and /b/. Then you could ask them what they think happens to the /d/ in *Good morning* (it changes to /b/) and the /t/ in *Don't you* (it changes to /tʃ/). Check by listening to the recording.

Answers

The letters underlined in tapescript 14 show examples of assimilation.

Optional activity

If your students have found this work useful, you might also like to raise their awareness of weak forms. This is another very common phenomena in connected speech in which many function words, eg prepositions, auxiliaries, pronouns, modal verbs and the verb *to be*, often have a 'weak' and a 'strong' form.

The pronunciation of the strong form usually coincides with the spelling, eg *can*, and usually exists where there is emphasis on the word, eg *Yes, I can!*. In the weak form, which is more common in unmarked connected speech, the vowel sound is usually replaced by /ə/, eg / kæn / becomes /kən /.

You could write the following sentence on the board and ask the students to identify the pronunciation of the underlined words:

The trip to the City Museum and Art Gallery in Bristol tomorrow has had to be postponed.

The trip /tə/ the City Museum /ənd/ Art Gallery in Bristol tomorrow /həs/ had /tə/ be postponed.

Then ask students to look again at tapescript 14, or another tapescript and identify which words are pronounced in their weak form. Confirm the answers by listening to the recording.

Reading 1   p46

Aim
This is a jigsaw reading activity, aimed at encouraging students to be able to summarize key points and exchange information as they might in a seminar situation.

1 Ask students to brainstorm animals they think are particularly intelligent and ask them to rank these in order. Then ask them to give reasons for their choices. This will lead into the next question in which students provide information on any tests or experiments on animal intelligence they have heard about.

Table completion

2 Divide students into three groups and refer each to a different text on Animal 'intelligence'. Students complete their part of the table individually and then compare with others in their group. Remind students that in this case the rubric asks for no more than FOUR words.

Answers

	Text 1: Crows	Text 2: Dolphins	Text 3: Orang-utans
Organization	Zoology Department, Oxford University	Earthtrust	Smithsonian National Zoological Park
City or place	Oxford	Hawaii	New York
Main aim	make (simple) tools	dolphins are self-aware	communicate

Note completion

3 Students continue to work in the three groups above, following the same procedure for this second task.

Answers

Text 1
1 lift / retrieve.
2 bent
3 nine times
4 materials

Text 2
1 one-way mirror
2 their reflection
3 zinc oxide / mark / zinc oxide mark
4 man / humans and apes

Text 3
1 symbol
2 right / correct
3 a reward / rewards
4 ability to communicate

Then regroup students into groups of three, with one from each original group. They should share information without looking at each other's texts or notes.

Writing p48

Task 2 – Organization and coherence: paragraphing

> **Aim**
> This section focuses on the structure and coherence of essays with particular attention given to paragraphing. Skills are developed by examining typical Task 2 questions and answers.

1 Students read the question and then Strategy box to check the best order to tackle this task – *understand the question, brainstorm ideas, make an outline / plan, start writing*. The first three stages of this could be done as practice before going on to the next section.

> **Exam information**
> The sandwich analogy
> Students new to IELTS type writing tasks often produce essays in which a lack of organization is quite common. Though more complex models can be followed, this analogy and structure can be easily understood and reproduced by students. It is important to remember that a lot of marks can be gained in the IELTS exam from a text which has overall coherence and cohesion, ie one that is well-structured and easy for the reader to follow.

Introductions

> **Aim**
> This section emphasizes the importance of a strong opening paragraph in an essay by looking at good and bad examples.

2 Point out that the same question is being referred to and then ask students to work in pairs to read the introductions and judge which is the best and why the others are less suitable.

Answers

Introduction 1
• Too brief
• Rather simplistic: *you need to be clever to do this.*

Introduction 2
Virtually repeats the question word for word in the first sentence. This is a common feature of students' answers. Point out that they will not gain any marks for copying the question, so in effect it is a waste of time. The second sentence is a very general statement that could be a bit more focussed.

Introduction 3
• Clear opening sentence
• Paraphrasing of question (eg *judged* instead of *true measure*, *educational success* instead of *academic achievement*.
• Well-expressed sentences – simple and clear, range of structures and use of a linking word (*However*)

All these points are positive features of a strong introduction. Therefore this is clearly the best introduction.

The main body

3 In this sample essay there are three paragraphs in the main body. Students identify the topic sentence containing the main idea and then re-order the other sentences to form a coherent paragraph.

Answers

1   There are many people who leave school at the age of 16 yet go on to have successful careers.
2   This is often particularly true of people with practical skills such as carpenters or plumbers.
3   Although they may not have passed many exams at school, they have successfully learnt a trade or skill which definitely requires intelligence.
4   There are also further examples of people who have not achieved academic success in education.

Students then answer the questions.

Answers

1   carpenters or plumbers
2   practical skills or those who have successfully learnt a trade or skill
3   *There are also further examples …*

4 Students repeat the task, ie reorder the text to form a paragraph and answer the questions.

Answers

1   It cannot be denied that creative or artistic ability is another form of intelligence.
2   Musicians have the skills to perform complex pieces of music while artists can create beautiful pieces of work through painting or sculpture.
3   Such skills cannot necessarily be learnt on a course or from a book yet could be considered to be more 'natural' forms of intelligence.

1   creative or artistic ability
2   *perform complex pieces of music* or *create beautiful pieces of work through painting or sculpture*
3   This type of skill is a more 'natural' form of intelligence, ie one not learnt on a course or from a book.

5 Students read the last paragraph in the main body and then answer questions.

Answers

Sentence 1: *A final example of another aspect of intelligence is knowledge*
Sentence 2: *They*
Sentence 2: *learning about a subject independently*
Sentence 2: *dealing with a variety of real-life situations and problems*
Sentence 3: *such difficulties*

Conclusions

6 Ask students to read the introduction and main body again and then summarize the line of argument used in this essay. Then you could go through the model conclusion below with them.

Model conclusion

In conclusion, there is far more to the idea of intelligence than academic achievement. Skills and knowledge are important and give intelligence a broader meaning proving that it cannot always be measured by educational success alone.

This is a good conclusion because:
• the concluding paragraph starts with an appropriate phrase
• it is brief
• it summarizes (yet does not repeat in exactly the same way) the main ideas in the essay and finishes with a significant comment.

It could also be emphasized that a good conclusion sums up the main ideas discussed in the essay or concludes with the writer's opinion but should not introduce any new topics.

Suggestion
It is important to advise students not to use exclamation marks in IELTS Writing tasks as they are likely to be inappropriate. Chatty, direct questions should also be avoided, eg *What do you think?*

7 A further Task 2 question is provided, and to encourage good habits, students should first aim to understand the question, brainstorm ideas and then make an outline. Check comprehension and their thoughts on this topic in a brief whole-class discussion. Ask students to skim read the main body then note down the key ideas and supporting information in each of the three paragraphs.

Answers

Paragraph 2
Main idea: Does inherited intelligence from parents mean children are more likely to achieve?
Supporting information: Not always the case – supportive and interested parents more likely to mean success.

Paragraph 3
Main idea: Early childhood influences future success.
Supporting information: Parents are a very important influence in this period.

Paragraph 4
Main idea: Teachers have greater influence on a child's success in later years especially if child lacks support from home.
Supporting information: Teachers help with subjects, advice about career, provide support.

8 Put students in pairs or small groups, and give them 10–15 minutes to write an appropriate introduction and conclusion. This could be done on OHTs for easier whole-class feedback purposes if possible. Draw attention to the Useful language box.

Model introduction

It is true to say that family background is an important factor in a child's learning and academic achievement, but whether parents have more influence on their children than teachers is uncertain and in any case will depend on a number of factors.

Model conclusion

To conclude, it is clear that both parents and teachers can have a huge influence on a child's learning. However, in my view, positive support and help from the family provide a more significant influence overall.

Listening skills p51

Listening and writing simultaneously

This is a typical Part 3 dialogue between a lecturer and a student on an academic subject. Ensure students understand the phrase 'nature versus nurture'. As a lead in, briefly discuss which they think has a greater influence.

1 15 Ask students to read the notes they have to complete, and predict possible answers or word class, etc. This is not specifically an IELTS task, but it practises skills they will need in the exam and for academic study.

Answers

1   (just) born clever
2   influence them
3   2,000 words
4   environmental
5   results might differ / are different
6   reasons or evidence
7   according to author
8   next tutorial

15

[DW = Dr Williams; S = Sian]

DW: Hello there, Sian.

S: Hello Dr Williams – I'd like to talk to you about my assignment please.

DW: Fine. Come on in and have a seat. Have you started work on it yet?

S: Yes, I have – I've started doing some reading around and I've roughed out an outline of what I want to do, but I wanted to just check with you that I was going in the right direction.

DW: OK, good. So what have you decided to look at?

S: What really interests me is the idea of 'nature vs nurture' with regard to intelligence and looking at whether a child is just born clever, or whether their parents, teachers, friends – people like that influence them. Do you think that this is a suitable subject for me to focus on?

DW: Well, it's a big topic for a 2,000 word assignment. People have been debating that for years, and there's still no definitive answer.

S: Yes, I know. I've been researching in the library, though and I've found several studies that have tried to compare the effects of genetic factors and environmental factors on children.

DW: Well, there's no shortage of literature on this subject, that's for sure!

S: Yes! And that's my main problem at the moment. For every study that shows that genetic potential is the most important factor, there's another to show the opposite!

DW: The best thing to do is to choose a selection of research that shows a similar pattern, and compare that in relation to one or two studies which don't follow the same trends. Then try to analyse why the results might differ.

S: OK. Another question I wanted to ask you was whether I should include my own opinion?

DW: It's fine to do that, but be careful not to make your writing sound too personal, that is make sure that you back up any statements with clear reasons or evidence and don't forget to make reference to where you found that information.

S: What do you mean, exactly?

DW: Well, for example, if you say that in Australia fewer children from lower income families go to university, even though that is a fairly well known fact, you need to mention the source of that information.

S: You mean find a study that has shown that?

DW: Yes, and include the reference in your bibliography at the end of your assignment.

S: The bibliography – should that include all of the books I've used for reference?

DW: No, only the ones that you've directly cited in the essay. Put them in alphabetical order according to author – not in the order that you use them in the essay. Remember: you were given a handout on this topic at the start of term.

S: Yes, that's right. Right – thanks for your time. I'll go and get on with it!

DW: OK – goodbye. If you have any further questions or points you want to discuss, then we can cover these in your next tutorial.

S: Great. Thank you for your help. Bye.

DW: Cheerio.

Vocabulary p52

Lexical links

Aim
This activity should raise students' awareness of the ways writers link ideas in a text by using different lexical items. This is important when understanding a reading text, and a particularly useful thing to look for when matching paragraphs to headings. It should also help them in improving the coherence of their own writing.
Similar activities could be done with other texts that they read, to build on this exercise.

1 Ask students to work together and look back at the texts and underline words that have a similar meaning to the main word provided. There are at least three in each text but referencing pronouns are also acceptable.

Focus on the different nouns and elicit that these help the writer a) link ideas in a text and b) give variety to the text by avoiding repetition. By noticing these links, students can also improve the skill of guessing meaning of unknown vocabulary from context, eg the word *implement* in Text 1. As a more productive activity, students brainstorm other nouns that have a similar meaning to words provided.

Answers

Text 1: hook / implement (possibly garden wire)
Text 2: dolphin / creatures (possibly apes / a subject / they)
Text 3: carried out / conducted

2 Look at the tip box and check students understand the idea of lexical links and how they are used. Then ask students to read the text on chimp communication and replace the first sentences. They should underline the lexical links which helped them.

Answers

B **Chimps have language.** They can, and do, communicate with humans. There is a linguist chimp called Nim Chimpsky with a vocabulary of 125 signs, all used correctly …

D **The evidence is not in their capacity to stand upright or use computer touch screens.** The evidence is in the DNA. Instead of comparing digits, or spinal structure, …

A **At one level, he is reviving an argument about classification: what is it that makes animals alike, and different, and how do you logically group them.** But at another level, he is raising an argument about human links with the rest of creation.

C **So a small change in classification translates into a big one in moral attitudes.** If apes were reclassified as human, would they then be entitled to human rights? And if apes were classified as humans, would Homo sapiens be guilty of genocide?

Study skills p53

Using a dictionary

Aim
Many students feel reluctant to use a good learner's dictionary, such as the *Macmillan Essential Dictionary*, because of the lack of translation. However, a learner's dictionary will contain a lot more information than most bilingual dictionaries or translators, and will be a huge asset to study. These exercises are designed as a test for the kind of dictionaries your students tend to use, in comparison with a good learner's dictionary. If your students tend to prefer using a mini-pocket bi-lingual dictionary or electronic translators, this is a good opportunity for a discussion about English–English dictionaries. Ask your students to bring in the dictionary they usually use, either in class or at home, and see how much information it can (or can't!) give them.

Note: These exercises are based on the *Macmillan Essential Dictionary* but they should work almost as well with any good learner's dictionary.

1 Ask students to try and work out the meaning of the abbreviations through the matching exercise. Check answers briefly as a class, and then ask students to look in their dictionaries to find an example of each one. Elicit other abbreviations they find, and clarify anything students do not understand, eg ≠ means antonym. If students cannot find examples in their dictionary, it should indicate to them that they need something more comprehensive.

Answers

[C]   countable noun …
adj   adjective
[T]   transitive verb …
sb   somebody
[U]   uncountable noun …
adv   adverb
[I]   intransitive verb …
sth   something
abbrev   abbreviation

2 Now ask students to look up the words listed and answer the questions. Again, a good learner's dictionary should contain all this information.

Answers

1 7 (bright, brilliant, clever, quick, sharp, smart, wise)
2 *should* is followed by an infinitive without *to* / no tenses, participles. Questions and negatives are formed without *do*. The negative is contracted to *shouldn't*.
3 give, issue, provide an instruction
   carry out, follow, obey an instruction
   disobey, disregard, ignore an instruction
4 yes (three stars in the MED)
5 high
6 no [U]
7 formal
8 adverb
9 AmEng subway = underground train. BritEng subway = pedestrian walkway under a road.
10 if you are being honest.

An exercise on dependent prepositions is included in the Vocabulary section on page 156.

Dictionary focus p53

As in previous units, ask the students to find the words in context before looking them up in a learner's dictionary for more information.

abstract (page 47: … *whether these creatures could remember* **abstract** *symbols and then use this system to accurately label objects.*)

symbol (page 47: ... *whether these creatures could remember abstract symbols and then use this system to accurately label objects.*)

insight (page 47: ... *such evidence provides a significant insight into animal intelligence ...*)

essential (page 48: *The first and last paragraphs are essential in holding the sandwich together!*)

correspond (page 48: ... *as they touched a computer screen, a corresponding symbol would appear.*)

influential (page 50: ... *when a parent's input is most influential.*)

input (page 50: ... *when a parent's input is most influential.*)

lack (page 51: ... *if a child lacks support from home ...*)

capacity (page 52: *The evidence is not in their capacity to stand upright ...*)

Vocabulary recycling

Call my bluff with a dictionary

This game derives from a radio/TV panel game in England. Ensure students have access to a good monolingual learner's dictionary in pairs. Ask them to look through and choose two words that they don't know, but which they think are useful. At this stage it is a good idea to monitor carefully to check that the words they have chosen are not too obscure. Now ask them to write down three definitions for each one (ie six definitions in total). Each word should have its correct definition, and two false, but plausible definitions (which they could find from the dictionary). You may need to model this process for them on the board.

Arrange the class into groups of four (two pairs together). Each pair should take it in turns to read their word and three definitions to the other pair, who try to guess the correct one. A point is gained for each word correctly identified. The word and the definition should be noted down.

When each pair has given their two words to the other pair, groups can be swapped around and the game played again. At the end, ensure each student has several new words complete with definitions to put in their vocabulary books.

Content overview

Themes

This unit focuses on the world of work, including job applications, a profile of the labour force and worldwide unemployment rates.

Exam related activities

Reading

Y/N/NG
Matching headings to paragraphs
Labelling a diagram

Writing

Task 1   Comparing and contrasting data

Listening

Part 1   Multiple choice
Part 2   Completing a flow chart

Speaking

Part 2   A job you would like to do in the future
Part 3   Discussing job related questions

Language development

Language focus and Vocabulary

Future plans and arrangements
Suffixes
Contrast linkers/markers

Skills development

Reading

Scanning
Guessing meaning from context
Understanding information in tables

Study skills

Extensive reading and listening

Dictionary focus

Speaking p54

1 Draw students' attention to the picture and ask them to suggest what kind of job the person does or what job she might be applying for. Ask students if this is similar to the job they do, or would like to do? If they need prompts, you could ask them who influenced them in their career decisions – teachers? parents? a careers advisor? Or someone else?

> **Suggestion**
> This lead in is aimed at students who have recently left school. If you have a class, or individuals who already have careers then you could ask them instead to discuss how they chose their career, why it suits them and if it is very competitive to find work in their field.

In pairs, students do the Part 2 activity then ask and answer the Part 3 questions, changing roles so that each student has a chance to be 'examined'.

Listening p54

Multiple choice

> **Suggestion**
> In the IELTS Listening module, all of the texts are heard only once. However, point out that the answers to each question may be paraphrased, eg:
> *Why don't we make it a bit earlier – say half six ... I'll see you in the bar at 6.30.*
> Or the text could contain distracters leading them to answer incorrectly, eg:
> *S: Are you going to be a singer in a band all your life?*
> *J: ... but I think I'd like to go into marketing.*
> Tell students that listening for these distracters can help to eliminate some of the wrong answers in a multiple choice question.

Aim

This exercise uses a Part 1 text (a dialogue on a non-academic subject) to help students with multiple choice, and to raise their awareness of the kind of distracters that are common in the IELTS Listening module. Two of the questions in this exercise are picture multiple choice. Note that this type of question is quite rare, and only occurs in Part 1 of the Listening module.

Tell students that they are going to listen to a conversation between two students about what they want to do when they graduate. Draw their attention to the picture box questions and get them to describe what they see. If they have verbalized each possibility, this will help when they hear the correct one. Also look at the other questions and elicit synonyms or other ways to express words such as *graduate* (v) (finish university), *America* and *Australia* (the USA / Down Under), *a doctor* and *a singer* (a GP / a pop star), *6.55pm* (just before 7), etc.

Play the recording once and then allow students to check their answers together. If necessary play again, but remind students that this will not be possible in the exam.

Optional activity

After feedback, you could ask students to find the distracters used in the tapescript, by relating them to the incorrect multiple choice answers, eg for question 2, the distracter is:

S: Are you going to be a singer in a band all your life?

Therefore answer C – a singer – is wrong. Sally doesn't want to be a singer, but she asks John if he wants to be one.

Suggestion

In the IELTS exam, you do not lose marks for incorrect answers (you only gain marks for correct ones), so if students don't know the answer, it is always worth trying to eliminate one or two wrong answers, and guessing on a multiple choice question – remind them never to leave a blank.

Answers

1 D
2 A
3 A
4 A
5 B
6 B

(S = Sally; J = John)

S: Hi John, how're you doing?

J: Oh hi Sal, not so bad, I'm just looking at this poster, have you seen it?

S: No, what's it about?

J: It's a careers talk next week – now that Christmas is over, I'm starting to realize that it won't be very long before I have to start looking for a job!

S: It's only the first week of the Spring term.

J: I know, but think how fast the last two years went – we'll be finished before we know it.

S: I suppose you're right, it's a bit scary, isn't it? Do you know what you want to do? Are you going to be a singer in a band all your life?

J: No, I'd like to be, but my dad would kill me … With a degree in Business, I've got quite a few options, but I think I'd like to go into marketing.

S: That'd be interesting – you'll make good money too, won't you?

J: I could do, but that's usually after you've worked your way up a bit. What about you – do you know what you're going to do?

S: I really want to try and get a job overseas – <u>my sister and her two kids live in Australia, and I'd like to go out there</u> …

J: Really, that'd be great! I'll come and visit you!

S: Yeah, OK. Apparently, there's a <u>big demand for medics Down Under</u>. I need to get more hospital experience <u>before I can be a GP,</u> though. The main trouble is I'm not really sure how to go about finding a job. I mean, I know I'll have to look through the adverts, but I'm not sure where the best place to look is, or how to sell myself properly.

J: So, what are you doing on Wednesday? Shall we go to this talk?

S: Who's the speaker, then? Mmmm …, <u>oh no, it's Professor Davis</u>. I had him for a lecture once and he went on and on, and never seemed to make any relevant points at all!

J: No, that can't be right. Are you sure it was the same man? <u>Professor Davis is thin and quite bald.</u>

S: Oh no, this guy was fat and he had a moustache.

J: That's Mr Davidson – you're right, his lectures aren't the best, but apparently he does important research, and gets a lot of money from industry for the university.

S: Oh, as long as it's not him – I don't think I could stand two hours of that, again!

J: No, Professor Davis is from my department and he always talks sense. So what do you think. Shall we go?

S: Maybe – what's he going to talk about?

J: Umm, let me see – it says here that the lecture will cover looking for work and writing applications, including tips on how to impress your potential employers. It says that there'll be time for questions as well.

S: That sounds perfect, actually. What time does it start?

J: Says 7 o'clock here.

S: OK, I'll meet you here, outside the main hall just before seven. We can go in together.

J: Why don't we make it a bit earlier – say half six, and we can go and have a quick drink in the bar first.

S: Great! Listen, I've got to go, I'm meeting Tariq in ten minutes. I'll see you in the bar at 6.30 on Wednesday, then.

J: OK – see you then.

Completing a flow chart

Suggestion
When completing this kind of question, it is important that students understand the organization and layout of the flowchart – where it starts (this may be the top, but may also be the middle in a spider type diagram, or the far left hand side), and how it progresses. Ask them to notice the numbering, as the questions will always be in the order that they are heard, and this will give them a good idea of how to follow the chart.

2 This is a Part 2 IELTS Listening module text (a monologue on a general subject). Elicit from the students as a class, what they think a talk about finding and applying for work might include. Then, draw their attention to the Exam information box in the Student's Book and in pairs, tell them to look at the charts on pages 55 and 56. They should predict what kind of answers they are listening for. Make sure they notice the order of the questions.

3 17 Play the recording once through and get them to check their answers in pairs. Play a second time if necessary.

Answers

1 National
2 Agency
3 free/no fee
4 direct contact/contact company (them) directly
5 job description
6 reference
7 (a) covering letter
8 send (it) (off)

17

Hello everyone, it's good to see so many of you here. This is an important time in your lives – your first job is an important step into the world, and although it's not irreversible, it's important to try to make sure that you find a job that suits you and that you enjoy.

My talk tonight is going to be divided into two main parts: firstly, looking for a job and secondly, writing applications. Another important area is interviews, but they'll be discussed in a separate talk. There'll be time for questions afterwards, so if you could wait until then to ask anything, I'd be grateful.

Right – looking for a job. There are four main ways that you can look for work. The first, and traditionally the best, is newspapers and magazines. Papers will often run adverts for different types of job on different days, for example, The Guardian advertises educational posts on a Tuesday. Find out which day is applicable to you for each paper. Another useful source of adverts for work are magazines, for example, specialist industry magazines. If you don't already know what's available for your subject area, now is the time to find out! Where you want to work will also influence where you look. If you can be flexible and move house for a job, then use national newspapers and magazines. This will give you more choice about jobs. If you don't want to move, or have a certain place in mind, it might also be a good idea to look in local papers or in local editions of the bigger papers. In some areas, especially the bigger cities, London, Birmingham and so on, there are magazines of local job advertisements that are distributed free, often outside railway stations and major supermarkets. The second place to look for work is through an agency or a job centre. This can be very efficient, as you're actually letting someone else do some of the job searching work for you. Mostly, agencies will get a fee from your prospective employer, so you won't have to pay anything, either. Another place to look for work is the Internet. This is becoming more and more popular, and many companies will also encourage you to complete on-line application forms. There are lots of sites that advertise jobs, I'll be giving you a list of sites later. You can usually search for the kind of work and location you want. Finally, if there is a particular company that you're interested in, you could also contact them directly and enquire about vacancies.

So, you've found a job that you want to apply for. What next? Usually, you phone the company and ask for an application form and a job description. The advert will often have a reference number, so make sure you have that handy when you call. Read the job description carefully – is this the job you want? Could you do it? OK, you have the form in front of you – either a paper copy or on your computer – what next? Some good advice is to take your time and make sure that the information you give is specific to this job and not just general. Remember that this is the first impression that an employer will have of you, and they will probably have a lot of applications – if it is messy, or filled in incorrectly, it will go straight into the bin! Unless it specifically asks you to handwrite it – and some will – then word process it and make sure that there are no spelling or grammar mistakes. Fill in all parts of the application form – if you think it doesn't apply to you, write n/a, which means 'not applicable', but don't leave blanks. After you've completed the form, most applications will also ask you to include a covering letter. This is your chance to shine. Think carefully about the job and why you're the best person for it. Why are your experience and qualifications relevant and what personal qualities do you have that would benefit the employer? Don't be modest here, but don't lie – if you say that you speak fluent Spanish, and you can actually only say hello and goodbye, you're asking for trouble! Finally, it's always a good idea to get someone you trust to look at your form before you post it, maybe a friend, a tutor, possibly even one of your parents. They might spot something that you haven't! If it's all OK, then send it off, giving plenty of time for the post to get it there before the deadline. The main thing to remember is that the perfect job for you is out there – if you don't get the first one, just keep trying.

Right, has anyone got any questions?

Language focus 1 p56

Future plans and arrangements

> **Aim**
> This is the first of two sections focusing on future forms (the second is in Unit 10). It aims to clarify the possible meanings of different forms. When referring to future time, it is important the students understand that different forms are used depending on what exactly we want to say (ie whether it's an arrangement, or simply an intention).

1 Look at the examples with the class and use them to establish that we can talk about the future using more forms than just *will*. Then ask students to look at the extract from the tapescript and find examples of different future meanings. Students compare ideas in pairs before class feedback.

Answers

1 I'll meet you here.
2 what's he going to talk about?
3 the lecture will cover …
4 what are you doing on Wednesday?
5 What time does it start?

2 🔊 16 Students choose the best options, then listen to check. Finally, conduct class feedback and check understanding.

Answers

0 Are you going to be (this is an example of when *going to* rather than present continuous is needed because it is an intention but not an arrangement.)
1 you'll make
2 won't you?
3 you're going to do?

4 I'll come and visit you.
5 I'm meeting
6 I'll see.

There is further practice of Future forms in the Grammar section on page 151 of the Student's Book.

Reading skills p57

Scanning

1 This activity gives practice in quickly scanning a text for information. Remind students how important it is to be able to scan quickly and set up the activity as a race. Allow them to read the questions (but not the text yet) and underline any key words. Then tell them to read and find the answers as quickly as possible, and to raise their hand when they have found all of the answers.

Conduct class feedback, then ask them in pairs or threes to discuss what the salaries might be for these jobs. The most important thing here is that they realize which job is most challenging, has the highest/lowest prestige, etc. Note that PA (Personal Assistant) is the term usually now used instead of 'secretary'.

Answers

1 B (*at least 6 months' experience in a similar role.*)
2 A (*maternity contract for 6 months*)
3 C (*you must have a 2:1 or first in Business …*)
4 A (*fluent in French or Dutch …*)
5 B (*post distribution*)

Guessing meaning from context

2 In pairs, students match the underlined words with definitions. Monitor to check.

Answers

1 confident telephone manner
2 a stable CV
3 WP
4 2:1 or first
5 a team player
6 fluent in French
7 computer literate
8 flexible
9 a post graduate qualification
10 good communication and organizational skills
11 methodical
12 good sense of humour

3 Students then divide the phrases into categories. This will check their understanding and also give them another way of recording vocabulary. You could put them into new pairs at this stage, to give them a chance to peer teach new words. Feedback as a class.

Note that these categories are somewhat flexible. It's not very important that all students get the same answer, as long as they can justify why they have put something in a particular category.

Possible answers

Qualities
- confident telephone manner
- a team player
- flexible
- methodical
- good sense of humour

Qualifications
- 2:1 or first
- Post graduate qualification

Skills
- WP
- fluent in French
- computer literate
- communication and organizational skills

Other
- related discipline
- a stable CV

Reading p58

Understanding information in tables

> **Aim**
> While this lead-in activity does not reflect an IELTS Reading task as such, it is very important, particularly for the Writing module, that students are comfortable with interpreting tables and figures.

1 In pairs, students should look at the statements (ignoring the statistics for now) and discuss whether they agree with the statements or not.

2 Now ask students to look at the statistics. Make sure they understand what the figures represent. They should then discuss the questions in pairs.

Possible answers

1 The number of people who have a traditional view that a woman's role is that of a housewife and mother, who does not go out to work, has decreased significantly.
2 and 3 Students' own answers.

Yes, No, Not given

3 As usual with this question type, encourage students to read the statements before reading the text, and then read the text looking for evidence that the text supports or contradicts the information. Allow students to compare their answers in pairs and then feedback as a class. Ask students to tell you where they have found the evidence.

Answers

1 YES (Paragraph 1: *By 1999, the proportion had more than doubled to 55%.*)
2 YES (Paragraph 1: *Between 1976 and 1999, the participation rate for women with children under 16 grew from 39% to 71%.*)
3 NO (Paragraph 2: *labour shortages are forecast in a wide range of occupations, including medicine and health, teaching, and public services.*)
4 NOT GIVEN
5 YES (Paragraph 4: *organizations will need to retain and develop an increasingly diverse workforce, …*)
6 NOT GIVEN

Matching headings to paragraphs

4 As in the Strategy box, ask students to underline key words in the headings. They then read to find paragraphs which have the same key ideas. In feedback, ask them to identify similar or related words, eg:
1–C *Women underline{interrupt} their underline{careers} to underline{care for family}.*
… Marriage, maternity leave and underline{care of children} account for 62% of women's underline{work interruptions.}

Answers

A 7
B 8
C 1
D 6
E 5
F 3

Labelling a diagram

5 Check students understand what the diagrams show, particularly the vertical axes on the graphs. Then, looking back at the text on page 60, ask them to label the diagrams appropriately. This is a relatively easy task, but should help students to start to get to grips with looking at graphs and understanding the difference between number and percentage.

Answers

Fig 1: C
Fig 2: A
Fig 3: E

> **Exam information**
> Diagram labelling or completion may simply be a question of scanning for figures, but students may also have to do some simple maths, as in Fig 3, where the figures in the text are percentages of men and women who have taken a break in employment, but the figures in the charts show those who have not.

Vocabulary p61

Suffixes

Aim
An awareness of how different word classes tend to be formed can really help students when guessing the meaning of unknown words from context, particularly if their language background is non latinate. This exercise focuses on some common noun endings. There are further exercises on suffixes and prefixes later in the book and in the vocabulary section on pages 156 and 159.

1 Show students the examples and check understanding. In pairs or small groups, ask students to find other examples of words with these endings in the texts (Parts 1 and 2).
Note that if they include the plural *-ities* ending, they will find further examples in the second category.

Answers

proportion	disability	*attachment*
participation	minority	commitment
distribution	*flexibility*	retirement
population	continuity	development
occupation	employability	employment
information	majority	
projection		
combination		
organization		
obligation		
contribution		
interruption		

Optional activity

Select words which your students may find particularly useful, eg *information*, *development*, *flexibility*, *distribution*. Ask them to find other words in the same family, using a dictionary if needed.

Writing 1 p62

Task 1: Comparing and contrasting data

Aim
This is the first of three sections in this unit giving further practice in Writing Task 1 answers. Data is depicted in a different format for each section (table, graph, pie chart) and the activities consolidate the work done in Units 1 and 3.

1 This lead-in section focuses on the topic of unemployment. Students briefly discuss the questions before class feedback. It would be useful to have some current unemployment rate figures ready to inform students if possible.

2 Remind students that it is vital to read the description and to try and understand what the diagram shows. You could ask simple comprehension questions to check this, eg *What is the table about? What do the figures refer to? How many countries are shown?* Give students a few minutes to consider the three questions before feedback.

Answers

1 The year 2000
2 For example: Morocco highest rate of unemployment for both sexes and very high female rate (more than 25%). Netherlands lowest rate and very low for males. Belize has high unemployment rate for females.
3 The simplest way would probably be to examine each section, ie both sexes, males, females and also focus on the highest and lowest rates. Emphasize again that selecting key points and grouping information appropriately are key features of strong answers.

3 Students skim read the sample answer and underline any points that they suggested above. Also elicit key points that they could have mentioned, eg grouping of developed/less developed countries.

Language focus 2 p63

Contrast linkers / markers

Aim
Over the next three units, students will look at some of the most useful linkers, or markers: contrast, reason and result, sequence and purpose. A mastery of these will help to improve their written answers. However, it is important that students are aware of how to use them correctly in terms of form and register.

1 Elicit that all underlined words and phrases from sample answer show contrasts (or differences).

2 This exercise focuses on the use of the conjunction *but*, which students will be familiar with, before presenting some less common contrastive markers. First ask students to use *but* to form simple sentences from the following prompts and then put them on the board:

ran to the station/still missed the train
83 years old/still goes swimming
John intelligent/lazy

Then add the more academic example sentence in exercise 2 to highlight how *but* is used.

3 Encourage students to use the table from page 62 to write sentences, but accept their own examples.

Example answers

Although the male unemployment rate in Belize is not that high, the female rate is over 20%.

Over 20% of females in Belize are unemployed, **although** the male unemployment rate is not that high.

(*Although* can go at the beginning of the first or second clause in a sentence. There is usually a comma after the first clause. *Although* is followed by a subject and finite verb).

The male unemployment rate in Belize is not that high. **However,** the female rate is over 20%.

On the other hand, the female rate is over 20%.

Unemployment has not decreased. **On the contrary,** it has increased.

In some countries unemployment has decreased. **Conversely,** it increased in other countries.

(*However / On the other hand / On the contrary / Conversely* contrast ideas in two different sentences. These linkers usually come at the beginning of the second sentence and are followed by a comma. These forms are followed by a subject and finite verb).

Despite the unemployment rate being low in developed countries, it was high in some less developed countries.

In spite of low unemployment in developed countries, the rate is still high in many less developed countries.

(*Despite / In spite of* are both followed by a gerund or noun. They can go at the beginning of a sentence with two clauses or in the middle. There is usually a comma after the first clause. If the subject of the verbs in the two clauses is the same, the gerund can come directly after these forms, eg *He went to the party, despite / in spite of feeling very tired*). Students may find it easier to use the phrase *Despite / In spite of the fact that*, as this can then be followed by a subject and a finite verb, eg '*Despite the fact that* unemployment was low in developed countries …'.

4 Give students a few moments to study the graph and again check they understand the information shown. Highlight the fact that changes over time need to be described and elicit or suggest appropriate vocabulary and tenses, eg *rose dramatically / decreased gradually,* etc.

5 Ask students to complete the gaps with an appropriate word or phrase while referring to the graph.

Answers

1   rose significantly / However / fall
2   Although / similar / higher
3   Despite / increased

6 Ask students to write two more sentences. They can compare their sentences in pairs.

Model sentences

> From 1993 to 2000, the unemployment rate in Australia declined. However, in Japan it rose steadily. From 1992 to 2000, unemployment in the US gradually decreased. Conversely, from 2000–2001 it increased sharply.

Writing 2   p64

Writing: further practice

Aim
This section provides further Task 1 practice comparing data from different pie charts.

1 Students read the four questions and discuss answers with their partner before checking with the class.

Answers

1   In very general terms, the pie charts indicate that Tanzania's economy is based primarily on agriculture, while in Ireland the service and manufacturing industries are very important.
2   1999
3   Agriculture is the main source of employment in Tanzania but is low in Ireland. The service industry is very important in Ireland but only 14.2% are employed in this in Tanzania. There are no figures for those employed in energy and water in Tanzania.
4   Different types of employment could be grouped and then the data needs to be compared / contrasted. So describing all of the first pie chart followed by the second pie chart would not be appropriate.

See Model answer on page 161 of the Student's Book.

Study skills   p65

Extensive reading and listening

Aim
These activities aim to encourage students to expose themselves to as much English as possible outside class, and gives them some further ideas of where it is possible to access spoken and written English.

1 As a whole class activity, students look at the list to find out what each learner has access to.

2 Students work in pairs to identify which of the *available* list they actually use. You could also ask them to discuss how often they use each one.

3 Ask students to discuss the list further in pairs, and to give examples of any sources that they do have access to, and explain which they take advantage of and which they do not, and why.

4 Ask them to draw a similar table to the one in their books and encourage them to fill it in. Review this at regular intervals over the next month or two. Make sure that they are accessing a wide range of language, and in particular reading texts which are more academic and more challenging.

Dictionary focus   p65

As in previous units, ask the students to find the words in context before looking them up in a learner's dictionary for more information.

issue (page 58: *How do people feel about these* **issues** *in your country?*)

project (page 59: *Beyond 2015, the Canadian labour force is* **projected** *to grow at a rate of ...*)

notable (page 59: *The most* **notable** *increase in women's participation rates ...*)

retain (page 59: *... organizations will need to* **retain** *and develop an increasingly diverse workforce ...*)

diverse (page 59: *... organizations will need to retain and develop an increasingly* **diverse** *workforce ...*)

influx (page 59: *One of the most remarkable demographic events in the last half century was the dramatic* **influx** *of women into the paid labour force.*)

contradict (page 59: *NO if the statement* **contradicts** *the information.*)

proportion (page 60: *Increasing* **proportion** *of employees with both child and elder care demands.*)

expose (page 65: ***Expose*** *yourself to authentic written and spoken English as much as possible.*)

Vocabulary recycling

Vocabulary box activity

Put students in teams of three. Take three words at random from the vocabulary box. Give them a time limit (maybe three minutes) to write down one sentence that contains as many of the three words as possible, but still makes sense. Check/correct the sentences as a class, giving each team one point for a grammatically correct sentence, and one point each for a target word used correctly. Then choose three new words from the vocabulary box and repeat.

Content overview

Themes

This unit focuses on crime and punishment and the effects on modern society.

Exam related activities

Reading

Y/N/NG
Matching sections and summaries
Sentence completion
Identifying text type

Writing

Task 2 Evaluating and challenging ideas, evidence or an argument

Listening

Part 3 Prediction
Note completion
Matching

Speaking

Part 2 Describing a favourite school subject
Part 3 Discussing school and crime related questions

Language development

Language focus and Vocabulary

Crime vocabulary
Defining relative clauses
Reason/ result clauses

Skills development

Reading

Skimming

Listening

Listening and writing simultaneously

Pronunciation

Word stress

Study skills

Understanding verbs in essay titles

Dictionary focus

Vocabulary p66

Suggestion
Crime and punishment is a popular IELTS topic and this section provides some useful vocabulary. A lexical set like this is a good example of vocabulary that could be usefully recorded in a mind map.

1 Put students into small groups and ask them to try and match the words and definitions, then check as a class. Make sure students are clear about the differences between robbery, burglary and shoplifting, as these are often confused.

Answers

1 kidnapping
2 shoplifting
3 mugging
4 vandalism
5 robbery
6 burglary

2 Elicit definitions of *terrorism* and *fraud*.

Answers

1 terrorism (using violence to achieve political aims or force governments to do something)
2 fraud (obtaining money from someone by tricking them)

Aim

This exercise gives practice in using dictionaries as well as providing language students can use in the final writing practice in this unit.

3 Students work individually to rank the punishments. You could also provide students with other common synonyms for capital punishment (*the death penalty / execution*).

Answers

1 A caution
2 A fine
3 A suspended sentence
4 Imprisonment
5 Capital punishment

4 In pairs, students compare their rankings and discuss a suitable punishment for each of the crimes in 1. This checks their understanding and gives some practice of the terms in exercises 1, 2 and 3. For example students might say: *I think kidnappers should get five years imprisonment because …*

Note: there is more on crime collocations in the Vocabulary section on page 157 of the Student's Book.

Reading p67

1–2 This is another task to develop students' scanning skills. Encourage them not to try to read and understand every word, but to scan the text to find the information quickly. Then discuss with them briefly whether they have anything like Victim Support in their own country, and ask them what they think of the idea.

Answer

It provides a free, confidential service with emotional support, information and practical help to victims. (lines 6–8)

Yes, No, Not Given

3 Go through the instructions with the students. Ask them to read the second text to find the answers. Remind the students that 'Not given' means there is no evidence for this answer in the text (even if they think it it is logically true or untrue).

Answers

1 NOT GIVEN (line 2 says this is the crime most commonly referred to Victim Support, but does not mention other charities)
2 YES (line 4: *Most victims of crime want to talk to someone …*)

3 NOT GIVEN
4 NO (lines 6–7: *regardless of whether or not you have told the police*)
5 NOT GIVEN (The words *never … again* are not mentioned in the text)

Matching sections and summaries

4 Make sure students read all the headings first and encourage them to look for similar words and phrases in the text, especially in the topic sentences.

Suggestion

This would be a good opportunity to build on the work on lexical links in Unit 4.

Answers

A 6
B 5
C 2
D 3

Sentence completion

5 Students refer to the text again and find suitable words to complete the sentences, ie they cannot use their own words.

Answers

1 letter or leaflet
2 to talk to
3 very much affected
4 face-to-face and telephone (*face-to-face* is treated as one word as it is hyphenated)

Identifying text type

6 As in the Strategy box on page 68, encourage students to think about the style of the language.

Answer

B an official government report.

Language focus 1 p69

Defining relative clauses

Aim

This unit examines defining relative clauses (non-defining clauses will be examined in Unit 7). These are frequently used in academic writing and are an area in which students often have problems. The two types of relative clauses are often confused; hence they are dealt with separately.

1 Draw students' attention to the sample sentence and the relative clause and the relative pronoun. Elicit other examples of relative pronouns and then ask them to identify pronouns and clauses in the same way in the following sentences.

Answers

1 ... but Victim Support provides a service (which) involves talking to a specially trained volunteer.
2 People (who) are victims of burglary can be affected in a wide range of different ways ...
3 Those (whose) houses have been burgled may be upset just at the thought ...
4 Victim Support can also help victims deal with people (who) usually need to be contacted after a burglary.

2 Use these questions to check students' understanding of these key issues.

Answers

1 things: *which* and *that*
   people: *who* and *that*
2 *who* refers to a person, *whose* to a person's possession of something.
3 no.

3 Use this exercise with the whole class to check understanding of when the relative pronoun can be omitted.

Answer

Object

4 Students should work individually to complete the sentences and then check in pairs before class feedback.

Answers

1 who / that
2 who / that
3 which / that / none needed
4 which / that / none needed
5 which / that / none needed
6 who / that
7 whose
8 who

5 Ask students to read the passage once straight through and ask them if they found it easy to understand. Draw their attention to the relative clause in the first sentence and elicit why it's used. Then ask them to rewrite the passage using the other relative clauses.

Answers

Burglary is one of the most common crimes *which people commit*. Some figures show that up to one in six crimes *which are reported* is a burglary. Therefore, many people will be burgled at some point in their life. Some of those *who are burgled* will find it devastating, even if none of their possessions are actually taken. People *who commit burglary* should realize the effect they may have on someone else's life. In my opinion, if someone *who has already been convicted of burglary* offends again, they should receive a stiffer sentence.

There is further practice of defining relative clauses in the Grammar section on page 151 of the Student's Book.

Writing p71

Task 2: Evaluating and challenging ideas, evidence or an argument

1 As consolidation for the first section of this unit, pairs compete with each other by trying to write the longest list of crimes and punishments. Then ask them to complete the sentence before giving their views.

2 Students should read the sample question and then answer the questions in pairs.

Answers

1 In the future, prisons will have bigger cells with computers and be for learning and working.
2 The main criticisms are that they will be like 'holiday camps' and be a 'waste of taxpayers' money'.
3 Students decide if they are for or against these prisons.

3 Set a maximum time limit of four minutes for students to skim read the text to find out the writer's opinion. Then elicit comments about the standard of this sample, eg:

In general, this is a well-organized answer offering opinions backed by evidence.

Answer

The writer is for these prisons but against (or disagrees with) the views in the statement.

> **Aim**
> This activity will help develop the ability to evaluate and challenge ideas, evidence or an argument in IELTS Writing Task 2 questions. Firstly, by looking at some relevant language.

4 Students decide which of the functional categories is most suitable for each of the phrases. Students then choose a suitable one to fill each of the gaps in the sample essay on page 71.

Answers

Introducing the main topic to evaluate – 4

Challenging ideas – 1, 6

Agreeing with ideas (possibly to be backed with reasons) – 5

Giving opinions – 2

Consequences / results – 3

a 4   b 2   c 5   d 1   e 6   f 3

> **Aim**
> This section focuses on the importance of carefully structuring Task 2 essays, and the text is a good example of a clearly organized answer. Analyzing each paragraph in detail also helps to show how the writer evaluates and challenges the central idea in the question appropriately.

5 Work though the first paragraph as an example then let students complete the others.

Answers

Paragraph 2

Main topic:

Learning and working is a good thing, as are better living conditions

Phrases which give opinions and supporting evidence:
1. I believe that this will not only give prisoners motivation and interest, but also help them live a relatively normal life.
2. I tend to think that improved facilities and living conditions will have a more beneficial effect on the prisoner than the opposite.
3. For these reasons, I fully agree that changes need to be made.

Paragraph 3

Main topic:

New-style prisons will not be like 'holiday camps'

Sentence which challenges the negative view in the question:

Some people argue that these new style prisons will turn into 'holiday camps', but I am unconvinced that this would be the case.

Sentence which gives an example to support an opinion:

For example, prisoners would be getting both physical and mental exercise in this scheme and would not be able to laze around and do nothing.

Sentence that outlines another reason in favour of the new system:

Since this new system would give clear goals for prisoners, I am certain it is a more constructive approach.

Paragraph 4

Main topic:

It is worth spending money to develop these prisons as in the long term it will produce better citizens.

Sentence which agrees with the statement to a degree but then gives support of the new prisons:

Although such changes will undoubtedly be expensive, I still feel that it would be a good idea to spend money on developing these prisons.

Sentence that shows the writer's view of the consequences of the new prisons:

As a result, the level of crime might be reduced and we would be able to live in a safer world.

Listening p73

Prediction

1 Either let students work in pairs or put students into small groups to discuss the questions with one person taking notes. Note that in Western Europe and the USA, truancy may be much more common than in the students' culture, and that whilst truancy can involve children staying away from school with the knowledge and consent of their parents, it is usually thought of as children doing so without this. Elicit key vocabulary and give definitions *truancy*, *truant* and *to play truant*.

Possible answers

1. Acceptable reasons: illness, doctors / dentist, funeral
2. Activities: shopping, sport, visit friends
3. Students' own answers.
4. Student's own answers.

Note completion

2 🔲 18 Tell students they are going to listen to a radio programme on the subject of truancy. Before you play the recording, give them one minute to read the instructions and questions, then check the format by asking what they have to do in questions 1–5. You could also ask them to predict answers to one or two of the questions or ask them to say what type of answer is required.

Answers

1. life of crime
2. weekend
3. heavy fines
4. bullying / being bullied
5. schools

18

[P = Presenter; R – David Renshaw; L = Lorna Coates;
J = Jennifer Simpson]

P: Today on 'Burning Issues' we are going to discuss the issue of school absenteeism or truancy. It's been in the news a lot recently because of the woman from Oxford who was jailed because she didn't make sure her two daughters were going to school regularly. First of all, let me introduce my guests, David Renshaw, a government spokesperson, Lorna Coates from The Crime Reduction Charity and Jennifer Simpson, a mother of three from Oxfordshire. Let me start with you, Mr Renshaw. What is the government doing about truancy?

R: Good Morning. Well, obviously, children need to go to school. Truancy damages education, of course, but can also <u>lead children to a life of crime</u>.

P: But aren't the new laws about putting parents in prison rather tough?

R: Well, we have introduced imprisonment in some cases, and some people think this is too hard, but it does seem to work. Even the mother who was jailed said that it was a good thing for her children because they now realize how important it is to go to school. It's not the only measure we have, though. <u>Something else we are thinking about is 'weekend' prison sentences.</u> This means that the parent would only go to prison at the weekends, but could still keep their job in the week. <u>We're also considering heavy fines.</u>

P: OK. Thanks for that. Lorna, maybe you could tell us why you think children play truant.

L: Well, I must say that I think the government isn't looking at the reasons why children play truant – they just want a quick answer, and I don't think it'll be successful. Children miss school for many reasons. For example, they might be unhappy at home, or they might have friends who play truant and encourage them to do the same. Peer pressure like this is very strong in teenagers, particularly. <u>Bullying is another common reason.</u> Children who are bullied at school will often avoid going. I strongly believe that more research needs to be conducted into this problem.

P: That's all very well but can you be more specific?

L: Well, for a start, I don't think punishing the parents will have long-term benefits. Everybody needs to work on this together – parents, children, <u>schools</u>, the government and social services. It shouldn't be just the government sending parents to prison.

Part3

R: We are obviously trying to make that happen, but it's very difficult. For example, <u>in the spring, there were over twelve thousand youngsters absent from school</u>, and a lot of these were with their parents. Now, if children are missing school with their parent's consent, then the government needs to take tough measures.

L: Yes, but it's not always as simple as that, is it? What I'm saying is that we need to look at the reasons why this is happening.

P: Right. Let's look at it from a parent's point of view. Jennifer, you live in Oxford and have three teenage children?

J: That's right.

P: So how do you feel about this issue? Do you think that the parents are responsible for children playing truant?

J: Well, I think Lorna's right that it is a very complex issue and I tend to agree that you can't punish the parents for the child's behaviour. If a parent is <u>sent to prison</u> or fined heavily, this isn't going to help us to understand the main reasons why their child is missing school. <u>If the child is unhappy or depressed about something at school, this isn't going to help, is it?</u>

P: A good point, Jennifer. So what would be better?

J: I think the emphasis should always be on the child. You need to find out why he or she is missing school. Then you can make decisions on that information about what to do.

L: Jennifer's right and can I just add that this is the approach that our charity would advocate too.

P: <u>Counselling is another effective option.</u> Wouldn't you agree, Lorna?

L: Well, it's certainly a possibility.

P: Do you have anything else to say, Mr Renshaw?

R: I can assure you that the government is considering all of these points and I should add that nothing is definite yet – we are still at the proposal stage.

P: OK. Thank you all very much for contributing to this discussion. And on tomorrow's programme …

Matching

3 Draw students' attention to the Exam information box and clarify that they need to identify which speaker makes each statement. Emphasize that each choice can only be used once, and that there is an extra choice. They will have to listen carefully for clues to the identity, eg gender and introductions such as *Let me start with you, Mr Renshaw. What is the government doing about truancy?*

Play the recording and ask students to answer questions 6–8.

Answers

6 D
7 J
8 P (note that L agrees, but tentatively 'it's certainly a possibility') P

Language focus 2 p74

Reason/result clauses

Suggestion
This is the second section focusing on linkers. You could remind students of the work in the previous unit on contrast.

1 Ask students to look at the examples from the model answer and underline which linking words are used.

Answers

Example 1: as
Example 2: Therefore
Example 3: Since
Example 4: As a result

2 Students decide which words indicate a reason and which a result.

Answers

As and *since* are used to give a reason, explaining why someone does something or why a situation exists.
As a result and *therefore* are used to express a result.
As a result is used to describe something that is caused directly by something else happening.
Therefore is used when something happens as a result of the reason previously given.

3 Ask the students to choose *so* or *because* and use the sentences to clarify the complementary meanings of these two conjunctions.

Answers

1   so
2   because

4 While it is of course possible to use a comma after all of them, if we need to introduce a new clause, explain to the students that we should always use one after *therefore* and *as a result*.

Answers

therefore / as a result

5 Students complete the three sentences using appropriate linking words. It is important that students realize that there is more than one possibility for each answer. Elicit different options and stress that variety will improve the quality of their writing.

Answers

1   as / because / since
2   therefore / consequently / so / as a result
3   Therefore / consequently / As a result (note that this is a new sentence, which means *so* is not an appropriate choice).

Writing: further practice

6 Look at the sample question together and check students understand all the vocabulary.

7 You could get the students to do this in groups, if possible using a poster or overhead transparency so that they can compare their version with that of other groups.

8 Allow students to compare their version(s) with that on page 162 in the Student's Book. Remind them that this is just one way of doing it.

Pronunciation   p75

Word stress

> **Suggestion**
> Before starting, you could raise students' awareness of the importance of word stress by dictating a few common polysyllabic words with incorrect stress. Can they identify them?
> eg dictionary /dɪkʃənri/
>   definite /defənət/
>   acceptable /əkseptəbl/

1 Check that students have a clear idea of what a syllable is. If they are not sure, try using their names, local place names, etc as examples. Then ask them to identify how many syllables the words have.

Answer

All of the words have three syllables.

2 If students find it hard to hear which is the stressed syllable, give an oral model, over-emphasizing the stress, and show them how the word would sound different if stressed on a different syllable.

Answers

Ooo	oOo	ooO
punishment prisoner	suspension detention expulsion	absentee

> **Suggestion**
> Some languages have very predictable word stress patterns, eg Portuguese, where the stress is usually on the penultimate syllable. It is much harder to guess where to put the stress on an English word, and often the only way is to learn the stress pattern with the word. That said, there are some 'rules' which are worth drawing to your students' attention.

3 Elicit that the words all end in the sound /ʃən/ although spellings are different. Note that this is only one pattern in which the penultimate syllable is stressed.

4 Ask students to mark the stress pattern for these words and elicit that although the spelling is different *-tion, -cian, (-sion*, eg in *explosion* is also possible), the sound is the same – /ʃən/, and all of these, like the words in exercise 3, are stressed on the syllable before the /ʃən/ sound. The number of syllables in the word is irrelevant.

politician (ooOo)
situation (ooOo)
station (Oo)
examination (oooOo)

5 This is another opportunity to emphasize the use of a good dictionary. Ensure that your students have access to a dictionary that marks word stress. You could ask them to look back at the words they found in the suffixes activity in the previous unit (page 61) and see what patterns they can find. They should notice that *-ity* is also usually stressed on the previous syllable (*ability*), but that *-ment* is not so regular. (***P**unishment* / *development* / *attachment*)

Speaking p76

1 Students make notes for one minute and then take it in turns to practise this Part 2 speaking activity. Monitor and as feedback comment on fluency and accuracy. Also ask students to report back about their choice of subjects.

2 Students take it in turns to ask each other questions. Monitor and then provide appropriate feedback on the strengths and weaknesses of their responses.

Listening skills p76

Listening and writing simultaneously

Aim
This is similar to a Part 2 IELTS Listening task, (a monologue on a general subject) but the main focus here is to give the students further practice in predicting answer types and writing notes while listening.

1 Give students time to look at the questions and predict the kind of information needed, including word class.

Answers

1   Neighbourhood Watch
2   For example, 1) group of people, 4) and 5) names of crimes
3   For example, 2) a verb 8) noun

2 19 Point out to the student that this question states no more than three words. Play the recording for students to complete the form. Listen a second time if necessary.

Answers

1   (the) local people
2   move around (much) or move house (much / often)
3   community spirit
4   burglary   } in any order
5   vandalism   }
6   contact the police
7   you have time
8   house / home insurance

📼 19

It's very nice to see so many of you here tonight. I'm Constable Moore and I'm the Crime Prevention Officer for this area. I'm here tonight to talk about 'Neighbourhood Watch'. Can I ask how many of you have been involved with this before? Oh yes, a few of you – that's good. Well, for the rest of you, Neighbourhood Watch is a scheme set up <u>between the police and local people</u> and I'd like to tell you a bit about how it operates.

Basically, it's just common sense and community spirit. Fifty or a hundred years ago, people tended to live in the area that they grew up in <u>and they didn't move around very much</u>, so most people would have known their neighbours. They probably knew each other's habits – what times they came home, who their friends were – that kind of thing, and so it was very obvious if something abnormal was happening. If a stranger was hanging around, or if someone was moving things out of a house, usually someone in the area would see what was happening and would call the police, or take some kind of action. In these days, where people move around the country so much, <u>you lose a lot of that community spirit</u>. We don't tend to know our neighbours very well, and we feel a bit embarrassed to get involved.

Imagine this scene. One day, you see a large van outside your neighbour's house and some men carrying things out of the house into the van. Without any knowledge or information about your neighbour, most of us would feel too embarrassed to do anything. Meanwhile, your <u>neighbour's house is being burgled</u> and all of his possessions are being stolen in broad daylight!

<u>Another example is vandalism</u> – people might see someone smashing a telephone box or spraying paint on a wall, but usually they don't want to get involved or call the Police.

These kinds of things happen every day. A Neighbourhood Watch scheme aims to bring back a bit of the 'nosy neighbour' in us all, so that we'll know if we see <u>something suspicious, and feel as if we can contact the police</u>.

How much you do is really flexible. It might be as simple as keeping an eye on a neighbour's home while they are away on holiday, or keeping a look out for suspicious things going on in your road. If you have time, you might want to take a more active role as a committee member, or volunteer to write, print or distribute newsletters. It's really up to you.

Another major benefit of being in a Watch programme is that often insurance companies will lower your premium on your house insurance. Talk to your insurance company to check the details on this, sometimes you have to fit suitable locks on your windows and doors first – but this is a worthwhile thing to do, anyway.

Right – has anyone got any questions …

Study skills p77

Understanding verbs in essay titles

Aim
This section introduces verbs that are commonly used in academic essay titles at university, as well as in academic reading texts. Although these words are not usually used in the IELTS Writing exam, a clear understanding of the difference between them will be helpful to students in their future studies.

1 Many of these words are similar and students may be confused as to their meanings. Ask them to look at the examples and answer the questions. Encourage the use of a learner's dictionary.

Answers

1   *compare* – consider the ways in which things are similar (and possibly different)
    contrast – consider the ways in which things are different (only)
    explain – to tell someone something in a way that helps them understand it better

2   *evaluate* – to give your judgement on the value or worth of something
    describe – to give an account of what something is like (without giving an opinion)

3   *identify* – to say exactly what something is, or to explain a term
    discuss – to write about a subject in detail

4   You *justify* your opinion by giving supporting evidence or reasons for it.

2   Students look at the essay extracts and choose which is an example of each essay question type. Point out to students the kind of language that may be associated with each type of writing, eg linkers such as *However*, are used to compare and contrast. *On balance*, is used to indicate that both sides of an argument have been considered and an opinion is being offered, etc.

Answers

1   C
2   A
3   B
4   D

Dictionary focus p77

As in previous units, ask the students to find the words in context before looking them up in a learner's dictionary for more information.

systematic (page 68: *Numbers were too small to undertake a **systematic** correlation between the kinds of help given and the needs expressed.*)

priority (page 68: *… due to the kinds of offence which receive highest **priority** – burglary and violence …*)

constructive (page 71: *I am certain it is a more **constructive** approach.*)

challenge (page 71: *… you have to 'evaluate and **challenge** ideas, evidence or argument'.*)

deprive (page 71: *… this is better than **depriving** inmates of all enjoyment whatsoever.*)

consequence (page 73: *Do you know what the **consequences** or punishments are for truancy in your country?*)

approach (page 74: *I am certain it is a more constructive **approach**.*)

version (page 75: *Compare your **version** with the rewritten **version** on page 162.*)

scheme (page 77: *'Discuss the arguments for and against recycling **schemes**.'*)

Vocabulary recycling

Stress patterns

Give each team a large piece of paper. Take a word from the vocabulary box and write it on the board without saying it. Give teams a point if they can draw the stress pattern on the paper, eg for *constructive*, they write: oOo.

You could give further points for correct pronunciation; being able to put it in a sentence; giving a collocation or defining what it means, etc.

Content overview

Themes

This unit focuses on globalization and global markets.

Exam related activities

Reading

T/F/NG
Sentence completion
Identifying the writer's purpose

Writing

Task 1 Describing a process
        Sequence and purpose

Listening

Part 4 Multiple choice with more than one option
        Short answers
        Note completion
        Table completion
        Signposts

Speaking

Part 2 Identifying the topic
Part 3 Discussing issues related to globalization
        Identifying reasons for and against
        Balancing the argument

Language development

Language focus and Vocabulary

Non-defining relative clauses
Financial vocabulary
The passive

Skills development

Reading

Scanning
Skimming
Guessing meaning from context

Study skills

Revising and recycling vocabulary

Dictionary focus

Reading 1 p78

Scanning

Aim
This section introduces students to some of the main concepts of globalization and helps them to develop the skill of reading for gist.

1 You could start by eliciting a definition of globalization, or simply by drawing students' attention to the dictionary definition. Ask students what they think are the good and bad things about globalization.

2 Students work together to put the statements under the headings, with a positive and negative aspect under each one. Having completed this activity, they should then be in a position to discuss some of the pros and cons.

Answers

Global Communications: a (negative), e (positive)
Global Travel and Tourism: b (negative), h (positive)
Global Media: f (positive), g (negative)
Global Business: c (positive), d (negative)

Language focus 1 p78

1 This first activity aims to build on work done in the previous unit on defining relative clauses, and to raise awareness of the different functions of defining and non-defining relative clauses. Elicit the answers to the questions from the students and establish that the first sentence is a defining relative clause, as covered in the previous unit, and the second one is a non-defining relative clause, which is used to give extra information.

Answers

1 a
2 b

Non-defining relative clauses

2 Look at the example as a class and then ask students to work individually to identify the two ideas in each sentence. In a feedback session, show how rather than repeating the subject we use a relative pronoun.

Answers

1 Main idea: the big tour operators take most of the profits …
   Extra info: (the big tour operators) own airlines, retail chains …
2 Main idea: Trade is worth four trillion dollars a year.
   Extra info: Four trillion dollars a year is 1.7 million dollars a minute.
3 Main idea: A garment worker in Bangladesh would have to save eight years wages …
   Extra info: Bangladesh is one of the world's poorest countries.
4 Main idea: The local people benefit from jobs using their skills …
   Extra info: The local people would otherwise have few employment opportunities.

3 Ask students to work together in pairs or small groups to complete the rules by underlining the correct alternative. Feedback as a class.

Answers

1 can
2 cannot
3 cannot
4 are

4 Look at the example with the class and then ask students to write out the combined sentences. Monitor and feedback as a class. Make sure that students place the relative clause in the correct place, after the noun to which the relative pronoun refers.

Answers

1 Greater cultural contact has been encouraged by tourism, which has doubled over the last 15 years.
3 The banana, which is Britain's most popular fruit, is worth more than £5 billion in world trade.
4 Shima, who lives in Bangladesh, earns less than €1.60 for a day's work.

There is further practice of non-defining relative clauses in the Grammar section on page 152 of the Student's Book.

Listening p80

1 Ask students first what they know about these organizations. Depending on their background, they may already know quite a lot. Students then check their knowledge by matching the organizations with the definitions.

Answers

1 d
2 f
3 c
4 a
5 b
6 e

2 Ask learners to discuss why certain organizations might be pro- or anti- globalization. This may be quite difficult for them, and something that they may not have thought about before. A lot of support at this stage will help with comprehension of the listening text.

Answers

Pro-globalization: The United Nations, International Monetary Fund, World Trade Organization

Anti-globalization: (some) Trade Unions, Friends of the Earth, International Aid Organizations

3 20 This is the second time in the book that the students have come across a Part 4 Listening (ie, an academic lecture). Reassure them that this is the most difficult part of the listening, as they will probably find this challenging. Give them as much support before the listening as you can, ensuring they are familiar with the vocabulary in the questions and the question types.

Answers

1 and 2 C, D
3 global / world trade
4 motor technology
5 100 years
6 C

20

In the first part of today's lecture, I would like to introduce you to the topic of globalization. I will start by considering what globalization is. Secondly, I will explain something of its history. Finally, I intend to look at who the main players in globalization are, both for and against it, and briefly summarize their arguments.

So, let us begin with what may seem an obvious point. What exactly is globalization? A lot of people think it is mainly about economics, or increased global trade. However, it can also be seen as increased cultural and technological exchange between countries. Examples might be McDonald's in Calcutta and Japanese motor technology in Britain. Now let us look a little at the history of globalization. There is no agreed starting point, but it could have been about 100 years ago. Certainly, there was a big expansion in world trade and investment then. This was put back considerably as the capitalist world came up against the First World War and then the Great Depression in 1930.

However, the end of the Second World War set off another great expansion of capitalism in 1948, with the development of multinational companies. These were companies interested in producing and selling in the markets of countries all around the world. Finally, globalization really took off when the Soviet Union collapsed.

It's important not to forget the importance of air travel and the development of international communications. The telephone, the fax and now computers and email have all encouraged the progress of international business.

4 **21** Questions 7–9 are summary completion. Again, ensure students are familiar with the summary text and have predicted the kind of answer (word class, etc) that is required. Remind them that answers must be grammatical and spelt correctly.

Answers

7   environmental
8   tropical rainforests
9   (cheap) imports

 21

Turning now to the main players involved in globalization, we find that there is a clear division between those who are pro-globalization and those who are anti-.

The main organizations against globalization are the environmental organizations, such as Friends of the Earth and Greenpeace, who put forward the belief that globalization harms the environment.

In general, they blame global corporations for global warming and the depletion of natural resources. The most obvious is oil and gas, but there are others such as tropical rainforests, which are cut down for timber, and the resources of the sea, which may be affected by pollution.

Organizations which represent developing countries, including international aid agencies such as Oxfam, are also against globalization. They are concerned that the global organizations, such as the International Monetary Fund and the World Bank, are not doing enough to help the poor and, indeed, may be adding to their problems. Some are critical of the World Trade Organization. They argue that the WTO is making it difficult for poor countries to protect and build their own industries.

Many companies in rich countries also oppose globalization because they are worried that competition from imports will cost them money. A good example is companies that make clothing and shoes. These are among the few industries in which poor countries can provide effective competition with imports of cheap goods, because wages are so much lower than in America or Europe.

Lastly, some trade unions oppose globalization too. They say it leads to a lowering of wages and conditions of work in the developed and the developing world.

5 **22** Give students a few minutes to look at the table, and play the final section of the recording.

Answers

10   1995
11   182
12   business community

 22

Having looked at some of the anti-globalization arguments, let's now consider those in favour. There are, of course, many organizations in favour of globalization. Perhaps the most important one is the World Trade Organization, or WTO. This was set up in 1995 and has 123 member countries. It administers the rules of international trade agreed to by its member countries. The WTO's rules make it difficult for a country to favour their own industry over imports from other countries.

The WTO argues that the growth of trade between countries increases the wealth of everyone. Trade allows those who can produce goods most cheaply to do so, thus giving everyone the best possible price.

Another pro-globalization organization is the International Monetary Fund or IMF. This was established after World War II in 1946. It aims to promote international cooperation on finance and provide temporary help for countries suffering financial problems. The IMF has 182 member countries.

Finally, the United Nations, which was established after the Second World War, has become a promoter of globalization. It aims to promote a shared set of values in the areas of labour standards, human rights and environmental practices between the UN and the business community.

So, we've seen that there are powerful arguments and important players both for and against globalization. I'd now like to move on to look at some of the key issues for debate. Let us begin by considering the question of global inequality.

Aim

Understanding the signalling language, used to structure formal talks, will help students follow lectures, but will also enable them to structure their own presentations in a way that will make them more easily comprehensible. This exercise aims to encourage familiarization with signals or signposts lecturers may use in organizing a talk, in order to help students follow an argument.

6 Check students understand the concepts of introduction, sequencing and so on by asking for one example of each from the list. As an example, elicit a phrase that might be used in the introduction (*In the first part ...*) then point out that *I would like to* is also used in the lecture introduction to signal intent and is followed by *introduce you to the topic of globalization*. Let students work together to categorize the signposts. Check as a class.

Answers

Introduction – 4 and 5

Sequencing – 7, 10, 12, (note that these phrases also appear in the introduction), 11, 3

Changing topic – 1, 2, 6, 9

Concluding / Summarizing – 8

7 20–22 Play the recording again for students to put the signposts in order. This exercise provides an opportunity for students to consolidate their understanding of the text, as well as the signpost phrases. Explain that these phrases are also useful for productive purposes for their own presentations or any formal speaking, eg in seminars.

Answers

1 In the first part of today's lecture
2 I would like to …
3 I will start by considering …
4 Secondly, I will explain …
5 Finally, I intend to …
6 So, let's begin with …
7 Now let us look a little at …
8 Turning now to …
9 Lastly, …
10 Having looked at … …let's now consider …
11 So, we've seen that …
12 I'd now like to move on to …

Optional activity

You might like to get students to do mini-presentations on familiar topics so that they can practise using some of the signpost language.

Reading 2 p82

Skimming

1 Allow students to look through the statements and guess what the figures refer to before quickly skimming the text to check. Allow them no more than five to seven minutes for the skimming. Remind them that they do not need to understand everything at this stage.

Answers (in order)

1 8,000 million
2 25 million
3 80
4 43
5 10 million
6 150

True, False, Not given

2 Encourage students to look through the statements first and check any words they don't understand. You may need to pre-teach *exploitative*, although *exploit* was taught in Unit 3. Then ask students to read the passage to find the answers and check in pairs before whole-class feedback.

Answers

1 FALSE
2 TRUE
3 FALSE
4 NOT GIVEN
5 FALSE
6 FALSE
7 TRUE

Sentence completion

3 Before students start this exercise, make sure they notice the slightly different rubric, ie that they have to choose one or two words, not three. Then allow them to complete the sentences.

Answers

1 (personal) sacrifices
2 twice
3 tiny share
4 noticeable
5 cash
6 fair rate

Identifying the writer's purpose

4 Remind students that for this type of question they need to look at the text as whole, and use information such as the type of language, the layout and so on, and who they think the intended reader is. There is no specific advice given in the text, nor any encouragement to protest, although both these things may be implicit.

Answers

B

Guessing meaning from context

5 Ask students to look through the text again to find the words.

Answers

1 fluctuated
2 retailing
3 sustained
4 precarious
5 undermining
6 declining

Vocabulary p84

1 Instead of simply matching words and definitions, you could give half the students words 1–5, which are all nouns, and the other half words 6–10, which are all people. They could check their answers and then teach their words to someone from the other group.

Answers

1 *funds* – available money
2 *commodity* – something that can be bought and sold
3 *retail price* – how much something costs to buy in a shop
4 *market price* – how much something costs to buy in large quantities
5 *income* – money that someone gets from working
6 *middleman* – a person or company that buys from producers and sells to customers at a profit.
7 *loan shark* – someone who lends money to people at a very high rate of interest
8 *trader/dealer* – someone who buys and sells things
9 *consumer* – someone who buys something or uses services
10 *player* – a person or organization that influences a situation, especially in business or politics

| **Aim**
This exercise aims at encouraging students to notice useful language they could use productively in a writing text.

2 Ask students to divide the phrases into the three categories.

Answers

Prices going down:
1 world price fell by 50%
2 reduction in the supermarket price of coffee
4 a fall of 20%
Prices staying the same:
3 prices remained stable
7 sustained its price
Prices going up:
5 the market picked up
6 market price of coffee rose by 50%

There is an exercise on verb and noun collocations related to business and money in the Vocabulary section on page 157 of the Student's Book.

Language focus 2 p85

The passive

1 Point out to students that the passive is used much more commonly in academic English than in general English. However, it should not be overused, especially in spoken English. After a brief discussion on the content of the facts, ask students if they can identify examples of the passive.

Answers

Paragraph 1: is derived, was known
Paragraph 2: was used, were fermented
Paragraph 3: is grown
Paragraph 4: is produced
Paragraph 5: is removed, is removed

2 Check students know how to form the passive (subj + verb *to be* + past participle) by asking them to complete the table. Make sure they understand that it can be any form of the verb *to be*, as the examples in the text are only past and present simple. You could elicit examples in other tenses and aspects.

Answers

Past simple: … was grown
Past continuous: … was being grown
Present perfect simple: … has been grown

3 Elicit that the fourth paragraph includes an agent – *Brazil*. Explain that an agent is the 'doer' of the action and refer students to the Grammar reference on page 152 in the Student's Book for an explanation on when an agent may not be needed.

Answers

1 Brazil
2 See page 152.

4 Elicit from students that the second sentence focuses more attention on the 'doer' and the first more attention on the process. Point out that this is a common reason for choosing to use the passive.

Answers

1　b
2　a

> **Aim**
> As well as giving practice in the form of the passive within a suitable context – describing a process, this activity provides a model for the later writing activity.

5 Ask students to quickly skim the through the text first. Encourage them to always do this with a gapfill. They then complete the text using the verbs in brackets in the passive form. Point out that all the verbs are in the present tense, which is usual for describing processes.

Answers

1　is made
2　are sorted
3　is roasted
4　are loaded
5　are mashed
6　are added
7　is called
8　is heated
9　is blended
10　is tempered
11　is allowed

There is further practice of the passive voice in the Grammar section on page 152 of the Student's Book and in the photocopiable activity for this unit on page 120.

Writing p86

Task 1: Describing a process

> **Aim**
> As an alternative to describing data, students may have to describe a process in Writing Task 1. This type of text is quite common in academic writing, particularly in science subjects, such as describing a natural process or reporting on a practical experiment. This section will build on the students' increased awareness of the passive voice (covered earlier in the unit) and also review and expand their knowledge of sequencers which should enable them to describe a process more effectively.

Lead in by putting students into pairs or small groups, and ask them to verbally describe the process shown in the diagram to each other. Point out that it is important to understand what the diagram shows and whether it is a continuous process or a process with a beginning and end.

1 Ask students to find and underline six sequencers in the text on milk. General comments on the text and the use of language (passive voice) could be mentioned at this stage too.

Answers

Line 2: First,
Line 4: Then,
Line 8: Next,
Line 13: After this,
Line 16: Following this,
Line 18: Finally

Highlight the fact that this text is taken from an information leaflet and therefore is not strictly a sample answer – more detail is in the text than is shown on the diagram.

2 Students read the two extracts showing connectors of 'purpose' and answer the two questions.

Answers

1　*in order to* is followed by a verb phrase.
2　*which results in* is followed by a noun phrase.

3 Students underline the connectors in the sentences before adding the sentences to the text.

Answers

1　as – line 4 after *milking machine*
2　because – line 5 after *refrigerated containers*
3　and therefore – line 11 after *any bacteria*
4　so that – line 19 after *and shops*

Writing: further practice

4 Students work in pairs and use the verbs in the box to describe the diagram about sugar production as clearly as possible. Monitor and check language accuracy before clarifying any points in whole-class feedback.

5 The final section provides practice in describing a process, allowing students to use recent linguistic input on the passive, sequencers, connectors and non-defining relative clauses. Although this activity could be done for homework, it might be a good idea to do in class so that students get practice adhering to a specified time limit.

When students approach this type of task encourage them to:

- Write an introductory sentence saying what the diagram shows.
- Use passive verbs, as the main focus is the process, not who or what does it.
- Describe the stages of the process in order (or clarify that it is a continuous process) using sequencers.
- Add some extra information about reason, purpose or result using the linking words.
- Add some extra information using non-defining relative clauses.
- Check their answer carefully.

Answer

See model answer on page 162.

Speaking p88

This section helps to familiarize students with the format of Parts 2 and 3 of the IELTS Speaking module by listening to a sample answer.

1 📼 23 Remind students of the format of this section of the module. Students listen and identify the topic question and key points on this card. Then play the extract again to elicit general comments about the sample answer – it covers all the main points on the card in appropriate depth, is fluent, accurate and about the right length. A strong answer.

Answers

Talk about a successful international company you know (e.g. Hitachi, Pepsi Cola):

You should say:
- what kind of products this company sells
- why you think this company is successful
- how this company advertises its products

And also say whether your country produces similar products

📼 23

I'm going to talk about a company which is called Honda. It's a Japanese company <u>and they sell a range of vehicles such as small family cars, estates and sports cars</u>. They also produce motorbikes. It's a very good company and is well-known all over the world. I'm sure Honda products are common in most countries but I've heard that they're especially popular in Asia and Europe.

<u>There are many reasons why Honda is successful but I think one of the main ones is because it produces a new range of models every year.</u> I expect the company has teams of skilled professionals who design and create cars using modern technology, which means new models have many of the latest features. Another reason for Honda's success is that the models are often more economical than some of their competitors – in both price and petrol consumption. Honda also makes expensive luxury cars too and some of these are designed to be very fast. This shows that Honda products appeal to a wide range of people. The company is also successful because parts for these cars are usually very cheap and easy to get in most countries.

<u>As far as I know, Honda advertises new cars on TV quite a lot and these adverts often look quite stylish. I've also seen their products advertised in newspapers and on large billboards by the side of the road.</u>

In my country you see many Hondas on the road but these have been imported from overseas as <u>we don't really have much of a car industry</u>.

2 Having heard a model answer, students now practise their own versions in pairs. Invite a student to do the task as part of feedback and/or ask for comments on the topic.

3 The Part 3 questions are broadly related to the theme of globalization and although these questions might not occur in a real IELTS exam, the students have had a lot of input in this unit and this section should provide relevant speaking practice. Some preparation time could be given, students then discuss questions in pairs before whole-class feedback. Alternatively, this section could be set up as a group discussion or simulated 'seminar'.

Speaking skills p88

Balancing the argument

1 📼 24 Refer students to the Part 3 questions again and explain that they have to listen and identify which question the speaker is answering.

Answer

Question 5

📼 24

Well, there are clearly different ways of looking at it. Cheaper flights mean that more people can afford to travel. This has to be a good thing in that more people can experience different cultures and places. On the other hand, more flights cause more pollution and some tourist destinations have too many tourists and not enough clean water supplies, and so on. As far as I'm concerned though, the benefits outweigh the disadvantages.

2 Play the extract again and elicit answers to the questions. Establish that it is vital to give reasons, not just short or one-word answers.

Answers

1 More people can travel (as cheaper) and more people can experience different places and cultures.
2 More pollution, too many tourists and not enough clean water supplies.
3 Draw students attention to the tapescript on page 172 of the Student's Book so that they can answer questions.

Answers

1 … there are clearly different ways of looking at it …
2 As far as I'm concerned …
3 Elicit a few examples and refer to page 24.

Aim
In Part 3 of the speaking module, students often find it difficult to process the question and then quickly produce appropriate, extended answers. This exercise provides some useful language to help them in such cases and gives them a little time to think.

4 Give the class an opportunity to practise using these phrases by asking a few questions from the previous section (Speaking 3).

Study skills p89

Revising and recycling vocabulary

Aim
This section provides suggestions on different ways to revise and recycle vocabulary. The vocabulary load is particularly high in academic English and new words and phrases will usually only be retained if they are recycled and revised, preferably soon after having been learnt and then at intervals afterwards.

1 Draw students attention to the picture of the vocabulary cards and show them other examples of ones they could make and use to revise and recycle vocabulary. They can be made of card, or even small pieces of paper, and can have as much or as little information on them as is helpful to the learner. At the most basic, they may just have an English word on one side, and a translation on the other.

Suggestion
Students might also find it helpful to mark stress, write the word phonemically, add information such as dependent prepositions or common collocations, give an example sentence, etc.

Suggested answers

1 The easiest way to use them is to look at the English word, and try to remember what it means, before checking on the back. Slightly more challenging is to look at the definition/translation and try to remember the word in English.

2 The beauty of these cards is that they are small, and can be carried around in a bag, or a pocket. Consequently, anytime that the learner has a few minutes, eg on a bus, waiting in a queue, before class, etc, they can be brought out and looked at. They can be discarded and replaced with new words on cards, as the learner can reliably remember them.

2 Students look at the vocabulary items and then how they have been categorized. These words fit quite neatly into three categories. Ask students to categorize the words from in the box from the previous unit and allow students to pick their own titles for each category. It is the thought process and analysis here that is useful so encourage students to justify their groupings.

Possible answers

Words related to crime: victim, truancy, detention
Words that are similar in my language: constructive, detention
Collocations: clear goals
Positive words: clear goals, constructive
Words related to school discipline: detention, review

Suggestion
Inform students that using vocabulary in a meaningful way will help them to remember words better (as shown by research). Examples of useful activities include ranking, ordering, sorting, etc.

3 Ask students to look at the four suggestions and discuss if they use these ideas, if they think they might be helpful, what other methods they use, etc.

Dictionary focus p89

As in previous units, ask the students to find the words in context before looking them up in a learner's dictionary for more information.

key (page 80: *The **key** arguments for and against globalization.*)
symptom (page 83: *The farmers need for a quick sale is a **symptom** of their inability to get loans at a fair price …*)
impact (page 83: *This had a devastating **impact** on their already precarious existence …*)
prior (page 83: *…to pay for fertilizers, harvest labour and basic living costs **prior** to the harvest.*)
decline (page 83: *Evidence of low and **declining** living standards is clear.*)
suffer (page 83: *When the world price fell by 50% during 1989, farmers **suffered** an immediate fall in their incomes …*)
reveal (page 83: *An examination of the price paid to a farmer … **reveals** that both have lost out …*)
maintain (page 84: ***maintained** or kept (para G).*)

Vocabulary recycling

Categories

Group students into teams of three. Ask them to sort the words from the Dictionary focus into 3–4 categories, as suggested in the Study skills above. They should write down the titles of their categories, and these can be compared as a class.

Alternatively, they could try, in groups to find categories for 6–10 words on cards from the vocabulary box, ie each group will have different words, and then justify these to another group, who should try to disagree.

Content overview

Themes

The topic of the unit is health and the way this may be affected by old and new techniques.

Exam related activities

Reading

Classification
Multiple choice
Matching headings and note taking

Writing

Task 2 Expressing your opinion
Giving reasons to support your opinions

Listening

Part 3 Multiple choice

Speaking

Part 2 Activities to keep fit or healthy
Part 3 Discussing questions on health

Language development

Language focus and Vocabulary

Medical vocabulary
Real conditionals
Avoiding repetition
Unreal conditionals

Skills development

Reading

Jigsaw reading

Writing

Using adverbs

Pronunciation

Intonation

Study skills

Editing 1

Dictionary focus

Reading p90

1 Ask students to use the dictionary definition to elicit the difference(s) between conventional and alternative medicine.

2 Put students into pairs and ask them to decide which statements they think are conventional or alternative therapies. Note that the concept 'alternative medicine' is taken from a Western perspective and that many of the methods referred to may well be more common in certain cultures, eg Chinese.

Suggested answers

Conventional: 1, 3, 4
Alternative: 2, 5, 6

3 Ask students to discuss the question in pairs and/or as a class.

Classification

4 Students may ask for the meanings of the four types of alternative therapy before reading, but these will become clear from the text. Ask the students to look through the descriptions and then read the text to find out which therapies are being described. Point out that classification is similar to matching. However, the headings or classifications can be used more than once.

Answers

1 I (*This therapy was invented in the early nineteenth century by …*)
2 A (*… originating in China more than 2,000 years ago.*)
3 A (*… patients treated with acupuncture … had less intense pain than patients who received a placebo.*)
4 C (*A chiropractor manipulates joints …*)
5 I (*… the eye marking can reveal a complete history of past illnesses.*)
6 R (*… the therapeutic manipulation of the hands and feet …*)

Multiple choice

5 Ask students to read the options carefully and then look in the text to find evidence for their choices.

> **Suggestion**
> Many of these multiple choice questions are based on the opinions of key people in the text. Encourage the students to look for and underline their names as a way of finding the answers, but make sure they check carefully by reading the sentences around the names.

Answers

1 D (*But there is good evidence that it does not work for … weight loss.*)
2 B (*There is no scientific support for these assertions.*)
3 D (*It works … mainly in the short term.*)
4 B (*Patients and therapists should be discouraged from using this method.*)
5 D

6 In small groups, students discuss which of the methods described in the text they would be willing to try and why/why not. They can also talk about the techniques which they have experienced.

7 Ask students to describe other alternative therapies they may have experienced, eg aromatherapy, etc.

Vocabulary p92

> **Suggestion**
> If a fair amount of this vocabulary is likely to be unknown, you may prefer to do the vocabulary work before reading the text. Unless you want to make the students have the experience that is close to the exam itself.

1 In pairs, ask students to use their knowledge to label the diagrams.

Answers

1 pupil
2 neck
3 lungs
4 back
5 spine
6 hands
7 feet

2 Students work in pairs to match the verbs with their definitions. Then check as a class.

Answers

1 e
2 b
3 a
4 d
5 c

There is an activity focusing on dependent prepositions on the theme of alternative medicine in the Vocabulary section on page 157 of the Student's Book.

Language focus 1 p93

Real conditionals

1 Look at the example of a real conditional in the table. Students may also know this as a zero conditional. Then ask students to read the text. You could set some simple comprehension questions: *What are the symptoms of the common cold? How long does it usually last? How is the illness spread? Should you see a doctor if you catch a cold?*

2 Ask students to look at the underlined examples and use them to answer the questions in pairs. Feedback as a class.

Answers

1 present tense (*If you have a cold*) or present perfect (*If you have caught a cold*)
2 present tense (*recovery takes place*) or *will* (or another modal) + inf (*the infection will be spread, It may also be spread*)
3 *Unless*. This means if something doesn't happen.
   When. This is not really conditional because it implies this always happens.
   Provided. This is used only if a particular thing happens
4 Yes, you can change the order. See *It may also be spread by hand if someone has the virus …*. In this case there is no comma between the clauses.

3 Look at the examples together and use them to further check understanding of the use of *provided* and *unless*. Also ask students to reverse the clauses and to use the present perfect in the *if* clause, eg *You'll / You may be able to go back to work if your temperature has dropped*. Then ask them to write their own sentences using the other prompts.

There is further practice of real conditional forms in the Grammar section on page 152–153 of the Student's Book.

Pronunciation p94

Intonation

Aim

One of the difficulties that many students experience is due to different intonation patterns in their L1, and they are unaware of the effect their intonation, or lack of it, is having on their English. Flat intonation, for example, may result in native English speakers perceiving them as bored and/or boring. Using the wrong intonation can give offence, as it is often used to show attitude. Intonation is also used to signal some aspects of meaning, for example, whether information is new or shared. It can be a difficult area to teach, but there are some generalized rules which students can learn, and thus gain some awareness of the importance of intonation. In these exercises, two fairly straightforward and predictable intonation patterns are introduced.

1 Students predict the intonation patterns in the two sentences. You may like to model the language for them. Give class feedback and drill the correct intonation patterns.

Answers

The speaker's voice should rise in the first clause (unfinished thought) and fall in the second (to show completion). This indicates that the first clause is shared information, and the second is new or additional.

2 Using the first exercise as a model, students mark with arrows the rising and falling patterns of these sentences.

3 [image] 25 Listen to the recording and ask students to check their answers.

Note that in conditional sentences, it is usual for the conditional clause to contain shared information, and to therefore carry a fall rise intonation, but this is not necessarily the case. Compare:

If your temperature remains high, you won't be able to go back to work.

We both know that you have a high temperature, and the new information is that you may not be able to go back to work.

If your temperature remains high, you won't be able to go back to work.

In this example, the idea that the temperature might remain high is the new information. It would be more useful in this case to reverse the clauses.

Suggestion

When practising intonation in class, it is often a good idea for you and your students to exaggerate the rise, fall and pause. Any change in intonation is often perceived as embarrassing by students, and they will probably be reluctant to change it very much. Hearing and producing differences that are large in comparison to their usual pronunciation may help to improve this, if only slightly.

4 The intonation of lists is another pattern which is fairly uniform and easily understood. Students look at the example sentence and mark the intonation. Again, you may need to model the sentence for them.

Answers

The speaker's voice rises on *reflexology*, *acupuncture* and *herbal medicine*, signalling an unfinished list, and falls on *massage*, signalling completion. Remind students that incomplete utterances usually have a rising intonation, whilst completed ones have a falling intonation.

Aim

This exercise is designed to show students the effect that a rather mono-tonal intonation has on native speakers.

5 26 Play the recording once for gist and ask students: *What are the lecturer and the student discussing?* Then play the recording again to focus on the intonation of the student and the feelings of the lecturer.

Answers

The student's intonation is very flat, and the lecturer sounds progressively more irritated, because the student is perceived as sounding uninterested, possibly even rude.

[image] 26

[S = Student; L = Lecturer]

S: Hello, you wanted to see me?

L: Hi, yes, I just wanted to see how you're getting along with your assignments this term.

S: I'm doing fine. I've finished the first assignment and I'm working on the second one now.

L: Good. Are you managing to find enough material?

S: Yes, I've been using the college library, the department library and the internet.

L: Fine. And you're managing to work to the deadlines?

S: Yeah, and I've been told that if I need an extension, I can ask for one.

L: OK. Good, you seem to be on the right track, then.

6 🔊 27 Ask students to look at the tapescript and as you play the recording, students mark the intonation patterns on it using arrows. The fall-rise/rise-fall patterns are included in the key, but it will be sufficient for students to notice an overall rise or fall.

Answers

In this conversation, the intonation is more normal, and the student gets a much more friendly and positive response from the lecturer.

S: Hello, you wanted to see me?

L: Hi, yes, I just wanted to see how you're getting along

with your assignments this term.

S: I'm doing fine. I've finished the first assignment and

I'm working on the second one now.

L: Good. Are you managing to find enough material?

S: Yes, I've been using the college library, the

department library and the Internet.

L: Fine. And you're managing to work to the deadlines?

S: Yeah, and I've been told that if I need an extension, I

can ask for one.

L: OK. Good, you seem to be on the right track, then.

Speaking p94

Students work in pairs as normal, but as a different approach, student responses could be recorded on tape (or even on video) and peer feedback given before the teacher comments. Alternatively, students could transcribe and evaluate their own recorded response before looking at ways to improve.

Note that the fourth Part 3 question relates to the writing task in the next section.

Writing p95

Expressing your opinion

Aim

Although strong IELTS answers do not always need to be in a formal academic style, they do need to be balanced, well-argued and well-expressed. Impersonal phrases (*It is often said ...*, *many people believe that ...*) are often regarded as more appropriate in academic essays than personalized sentences. However, it should be stressed that generally,

in an IELTS Task 2 answer, personal phrases such as *I strongly believe ...* or *In my view ...* are acceptable. This section focuses on developing a more academic style.

1 Students read all the phrases then divide them into the three categories. After the activity, emphasize that giving first person advice, using rhetorical questions, contractions or question tags (see tip box) is not usually appropriate when writing academic essays.

Answers

1 C – use of direct question is inappropriate in writing
2 A – appropriate use of impersonal style
3 B – personal opinion using 'I' but appropriate in an IELTS Task 2 essay
4 A – appropriate use of impersonal style.
5 B – personal opinion using 'I' but appropriate in an IELTS Task 2 essay
6 C – use of rhetorical question and informal expression inappropriate in writing

Giving reasons to support your opinions

2 Point out that giving reasons for opinions is very important to get a good mark in the IELTS exam and then ask students to match the views on the left with the reasons on the right. Key words that reveal the links between each of the texts could be examined.

Answers

1 d
2 a
3 b
4 c

3 Write the example sentence on the board and invite comments. Go through the example opinion and then allow students to work in pairs and state their opinions (with reasons) using appropriate language on each of the four statements.

Note that more personal expressions are likely to surface in this context and this would be acceptable as spoken English, but encourage use of more impersonal phrases too. This exercise could develop into a more in-depth class discussion.

Using adverbs

4 This section offers another way for students to express their opinions more indirectly. Ask students to look at the adverbs in the box and match them with the questions. Then ask students to use them in the gap-fill exercise. As above, they should do this individually, and then compare and discuss their answers.

1 apparently
2 unfortunately
3 fortunately
4 surprisingly
5 naturally, clearly, obviously

5 For this exercise, the answer will largely depend on the student's opinion. However, only the answers that are possible are included below.

Answers

1 naturally, clearly, obviously
2 naturally, clearly, obviously, unfortunately, fortunately, apparently
3 apparently, unfortunately
4 unfortunately, naturally, clearly, obviously
5 apparently, surprisingly
6 surprisingly, apparently, clearly, obviously

> **Suggestion**
> Although adverbs can come in different places in a sentence, for example, follow the subject, for the sake of ease and clarity students could be encouraged to always use them in this way at the beginning of a sentence, as in this exercise.

6 This section gives further writing practice of IELTS Writing Task 2. Ask students read the question and underline key words. Allow them plenty of time to consider how much they agree with the statement. Note that students may feel that they have to have a single opinion. Emphasize that a balanced argument and an opinion is what is required. There are many examples of both positive and negative arguments for alternative medicine in the previous exercises. Encourage them to use these, and remind them of the work they have just completed on expressing an opinion.

They may want to brainstorm in pairs or small groups before planning their essay, following the guide given. The essay may be written as a timed piece of work in class, or given for homework to complete. See model answer on page 163 of the Student's Book.

Reading skills p97

Matching headings and note taking

> **Aim**
> These reading skills exercises practise skills which will be useful in the IELTS exam. It is designed as a jigsaw activity to give students more of a real reason to read and take notes.

1 Divide students into two groups. Ask group A to read the first text and match the paragraphs with the headings, and group B do the same with the second one. Let them check together.

Answers

Genetically modified animals:
A What are GM animals?
B What else could GM animals be used for?
C Is this safe for humans?
D What about the animals?

Human cloning:
A What exactly is cloning?
B How is it done?
C Is it legal?
D Why might people want to clone humans?
E Why ban cloning?

2 Still in the same groups, ask students to work together to make notes on their text.

3 Put students in new pairs, with someone who read the other text. They should then tell each other about their texts and exchange opinions.

Listening p98

> **Suggestion**
> This text is similar to that in an IELTS Listening module Part 3, and includes four speakers in a seminar situation. One of the big difficulties for students in this kind of text is identifying all of the speakers. Point out clues such as gender and signposting of names by other members of the group, eg *What do you think, Alice?*

1 🎧 28 Before listening, elicit from the students some information about human cloning. Allow students time to read the questions and underline key words. You might want to pre-teach some of the vocabulary, eg *clones*, *infertile* and *liver*.

Answers

1 B
2 C
3 D
4 A
5 B

28

[L = Lecturer; B = Barry; R = Ron; A = Alice]

L: OK, Barry, thank you for your very clear presentation on human cloning. I'd like to start the discussion by asking you this. Even though, as you said, <u>therapeutic cloning could be used by hospitals to fight and cure disease</u>, whereas reproductive cloning is growing an entirely new human, do you think that ethically there is really any difference between the two?

B: That's a good question, and I'm not really sure that I know the answer. Reproductive cloning is often the one that people fear. If you ask me, the idea of making a new person who is identical to someone who is living, or has lived, is a bit too close to science fiction.

L: What do you think, Ron? You look as if you have something to say.

R: Yeah, Barry's right. People think of armies of clones, all the same, non-thinking machines, almost, who could be used in an attack by some mad dictator. There are so many books and films on this theme that people seem to imagine that it could really happen.

A: And couldn't it?

B: No, of course not, Alice. Just because you have the same genes as someone doesn't mean you're a robot. If that were true, then every set of identical twins would be doing exactly the same thing all the time, and that doesn't happen, does it Ron – you have twin brothers, don't you?

R: Yes, I do, and although they look the same, they have quite different personalities. <u>So, equally it's unrealistic to think that clones would behave in the same way</u>.

A: So is there a positive side to reproductive cloning? I mean, would anybody benefit.

R: <u>Childless couples.</u> As I see it, they'd have the chance to try for a baby, even though they were <u>infertile</u>.

L: That's a very good point, but we haven't touched upon therapeutic cloning yet. What does anyone think about that?

A: The possibilities are fascinating. Can you imagine being able <u>to grow a new heart for someone who needed a transplant, or a new kidney</u>, or a lung? We have the technology already to transplant these things, but often the problem is finding an organ. Usually you have to wait for someone who wants to donate an organ and who has the same blood and tissue type, to die. Didn't you do some research into this, Ron?

R: Yes, I was reading about this, and apparently it could also be used for some degenerative diseases – you know, like Parkinson's, that get worse as you get older.

L: So, are we playing God, here? What do you think, Barry?

B: As far as the ethics go, I think that therapeutic cloning is easier for most people to accept. <u>You're only talking about making a part of a human being, and not a whole one</u>, that can think, and feel and talk back.

Language focus 2   p99

Avoiding repetition

Aim

This section aims to raise students' awareness of reference in order to help them understand more complex texts, as well as improve the style of their own writing. As with the lexical links activity in Unit 4, similar activities could be done with any text they read.

1 Look at the examples with the students and check they understand the idea of avoiding repetition through using reference words. Having looked at the example, ask students to find what is referred to. If students do not wish to write on their books, you could copy the text to allow them to draw arrows from the underlined words to what they refer to.

Answers

this: something which should not be there
them: the lungs
this: dirt or dust getting into the lungs
them: the lungs
it: coughing
this: trying not to cough
it: trying not to cough or not coughing

A cough is a reflex action which happens when nerves are stimulated in the lining of the respiratory passages by something which should not be there. This may be dust, a piece of food, or phlegm caused by an infection. The lungs are normally a sterile environment, so if dirt or dust get into them this could cause them to become a breeding ground for bacteria and infection. Coughing clears the lungs. If it is painful you may try not to cough and this can be dangerous because it can lead to a chest infection and even pneumonia.

2 Ask the students to replace the underlined sections with reference links as shown in the example.

Answers

1   They
2   They, they
3   This, it
4   one, this or that
5   it, then
6   These

3 You could take specific examples from student essays you have recently marked (without saying who wrote them) or ask students to identify passages of their own to rewrite to improve cohesion and avoid repetition.

Language focus 3 p100

Unreal conditionals

1 Look at the table in the Student's Book and compare it with real conditionals table on page 93. Check understanding by asking students how real the situation is seen to be. Then ask students to work together to answer the questions. Check as a class.

Answers

1 A past tense (in this case passive)
2 No. Although they are using a past tense form they are talking about a hypothetical situation.
3 *Would* + inf (or another modal expressing possibility.)
4 Yes. Again the comma would be removed in this case.

2 Ask students to write some unreal conditional sentences using the prompts. Elicit examples in feedback.

Sample answers

1 If human cloning were legalized, people might live forever.
2 Infertile parents could have children if human cloning were legalized.
3 If a human were cloned, they wouldn't be unique.
4 If GM animals escaped into the wild, they might spread their genes.
5 If we made food from GM animals, it might be poisonous.
6 GM animals could displace wild animals if they escaped into the wild.

3 Now ask students to write their own sentences, either giving their opinion or simply using their imaginations.

There is further practice of unreal conditional forms in the Grammar section on page 153 of the Student's Book.

Study skills p101

Editing 1

> **Suggestion**
> While feedback and corrections from the teacher can be invaluable, students also need to learn to edit and correct their own work. This will make them more independent learners, as well as being a useful strategy in the exam.
>
> You may wish to use a correction code when marking their written work, for example:
> Sp – *spelling*; P – *punctuation*; WW – *wrong word*; WT – *wrong tense*
> This can help students to develop their ability to identify and correct errors for themselves.

1 Go through the identified errors with numbers first, ensuring that the students understand what the error is and how to correct it. These are errors that students at this level will commonly make, but will usually understand without lengthy explanations.
Then ask them in pairs to identify the other underlined errors. There are six.

Answers

See exercise 2.

2 Students correct the errors.

Answers

I am an international student **1** studying Business at (wrong word) **2** Plymouth University. I have been here for **3** nearly eight months. I believe (spelling) I am **4** suited to business management because I worked in my father's company **5** last year and I learnt (wrong tense) practical business knowledge from my father. I am **6** interested **7** in many things. I enjoy listening to (wrong form/word missing) music, both classic and pop. I very much like (word order) reading foreign novels because **8** it provides an opportunity of learning the (word not needed) English.

3 This is further practice of common, but quite straightforward errors, and good practice for editing. Ask students in pairs to identify and correct the seven errors.

Answers

If I will (word not needed) get a good degree, I am going to (missing word) work in my father's company again. This is a the (wrong word) best way for me to learning learn (wrong form) the business. I will work very hardly hard (wrong form), that which (wrong word) will please my father, and I hope I will soon be (missing word) promoted!

4 It will be more difficult for students to identify mistakes in their own work, often because the mistakes will be at discourse level, rather than single words. However, it is a good habit for them to keep a note of particular problem areas they have.

Dictionary focus p101

As in previous units, ask the students to find the words in context before looking them up in a learner's dictionary for more information.

involve (page 90: ... *involves applying pressure to neck, elbows, knees and so on.*)

represent (page 91: *'there is no known mechanism by which body organs can be **represented** ... to specific locations in the iris'.*)

claim (page 91: *Practitioners **claim** that reflexology can cleanse the body of toxins ...*)

subjective (page 91: *The researchers, using both **subjective** tests and objective lung-function tests, could find no evidence ...*)

overall (page 92: *Which of the following statements best sums up the **overall** content of this article?*)

appropriate (page 95: *Informal – acceptable in informal speech, but not **appropriate** in academic writing.*)

aspect (page 95: *Some people might want to combine **aspects** of conventional medicine and elements from alternative therapies.*)

ban (page 97: *Why **ban** cloning?*)

opportunity (page 101: *I like reading foreign novels, because it provides an **opportunity** to learn English.* Note: this is a corrected version of the context given in the exercise.)

Vocabulary recycling

Spelling test

Using words from this unit's *Dictionary focus*, and the vocabulary box, give students a spelling test of the more challenging words (perhaps for 10 words). Instead of giving the answers yourself, ask the class to mingle and check with each other any they feel unsure of, as well as checking they remember the meaning of the words. Monitor, giving individual help and give class feedback on any words that seem problematic.

Content overview

Themes

This unit is based on the topic of technology and focuses on robots, various gadgets and how a hot air balloon works.

Exam related activities

Reading
T/F/NG

Writing

Task 1 Exemplification
        Drawing conclusions
        Describing how something works
        Infinitives of purpose

Listening

Part 4 Note completion
        Multiple choice

Speaking

Part 2 Describing a machine
Part 3 Discussing technological developments

Language development

Language focus

Present perfect vs. past simple
Countable and uncountable nouns
Writing: exemplification
Drawing conclusions
Infinitives of purpose

Skills development

Reading

Skimming and scanning

Listening

Listening for main ideas
Information transfer – pie charts and bar charts
Listening and writing simultaneously

Study skills

Editing 2

Dictionary focus

Listening 1 p102

Aim
This is a Part 4 Listening module text, ie an academic lecture. As this is the most challenging part for students and as they only hear the text once in the actual exam, it is important to build their confidence in class. The first gist listening in this exercise aims to help students with this.

1 📼 29 In pairs or small groups, ask students to look at the pictures and discuss what they see. You could ask students if they have any contact with robots, or if they are interested in them, etc. Elicit or teach other words used in the text for robots. Play the recording once and ask students to number the names of the robots as they hear them. For feedback, you could elicit any information about these robots they may have heard, which will provide further preparation for the next stage.

Answers

1 Talos
2 Joseph Jaquard's textile machine
3 the Analytic Engine
4 Universal Automaton
5 Shakey
6 Asimo

There is a vocabulary exercise on synonyms for the word *make* that are used in this listening on page 158 of the Student's Book.

29

In today's lecture, I want to give you a brief overview of the history of robotics, from ancient times up to the present day. We can then look at some of the key inventions in more detail over the next few weeks.

You may have wondered when I mentioned ancient times. Aren't robots a modern invention? Well, technically, yes, but ancient civilizations had very similar ideas, for example, there was the story of Talos, a man made from bronze, who guarded the island of Crete, in Greece. Then in Roman mythology, the god Vulcan made two female robots out of gold to help him walk.

However, by 1774 myth had become fact, and two French brothers, Pierre and Henri Louis Jacquet-Droz were creating very complicated automatons, such as a boy robot, which could draw and write messages. They also created a robot woman, which could play a piano. Another example was a mechanical duck, which quacked, flapped its wings and pretended to eat and drink. This was invented at about the same time, by a man called Vaucanson. That's V.A.U.C.A.N.S.O.N.

In the next century robots started to be designed, which were not so much toys, but had more practical, industrial uses. The industrial robots used in factories today have their origins in these early automated machines.

A good example is Joseph Jacquard's Textile Machine, invented in 1801 which was operated by punch cards.

Then, in 1834, Charles Babbage designed one of the first automatic computers, the Analytic Engine. This also used programmes on punched cards, to carry out mathematical operations. It had a memory capable of one thousand 50 digit numbers. The project was never finished, but it provided an excellent model for later developments.

2 29

> **Exam information**
> In this listening exercise, a range of question types is used, as is normal in IELTS. Explain to students that listenings are usually split up into parts, and they will be given a short amount of time in the exam (about half a minute) to look ahead at the questions for that part.

Give students some time to look through the questions first. Check they understand them, pre-teach any vocabulary they find difficult, and encourage them to underline key words to listen for. If they have heard the text already they may be able to guess some answers. Then play the recording and let them check together before going through the answers as a class. Remind students that they may have to change the form of the answer.

Answers

1	France	4	1801
2	write (messages)	5	automatic computers
3	Vaucanson		

3 30 Ensure students understand that two answers are required here. In this question, both choices are worth a mark each. Play the recording.

Answers

6 and 7 A, D

 30

The 20th century was a time which saw huge development in the science of robotics, particularly after the computer had been developed in the mid-forties. George Devol designed the Universal Automaton in 1954, which was the first programmable robot. The name was later shortened to Unimaton, which became the name of the first robot company.

Unimaton Inc sold designs to General Motors, who, in 1962, installed the first industrial robot on a production line. The 'Unimate' robot was used in a car factory to lift and stack hot pieces of metal.

In 1970, a computer controlled robot called Shakey was developed. On one occasion Shakey was asked to push a box off a platform. It couldn't reach the box, so it found a ramp, pushed the ramp against the platform, rolled up the ramp and pushed the box to the floor. Doesn't that seem like intelligence?

4 31 Before playing the recording, point out that two answers are required for the first section, and no more than three words should be used for the second. Make sure students have read the summary carefully and predicted the type of answer and word class. Play the recording.

Answers

8 and 9	A, C
10	Japan
11	two legs
12	first non-human

 31

Since then hundreds of robots have been designed and developed for a variety of uses: assembling small parts in factories, providing the handicapped with artificial limbs, carrying out household chores and even carrying out surgical operations.

In 1967 Japan imported its first industrial robot from the United States, which was, at this time, about ten years ahead in robot technology. However, within a very short time, Japan started to catch up and then take over. Japan is now a world leader in robotics. Sony's Aibo robot dog was the first sophisticated robotic product to really sell well to the public. Now Honda have created Asimo, who has been made two legged, in order to look more human. He is designed as 'a partner for people', or to work in the home. <u>Asimo became the first non-human to open the New York Stock Exchange.</u> Asimo will continue to be developed and, in the future, its power may come from hydrogen fuel cells, a technology whose only waste product is water. This may mean that Asimo will have to go to the toilet!

If these plans work out then society in the future could be very different. In fifty years time, perhaps, no home or workplace will be without one.

Language focus 1 p103

Present perfect vs. past simple

Suggestion
Although students at this level can usually produce the present perfect, they may still have problems knowing when to use it appropriately. Looking at examples in texts they read can help build their understanding.

Aim
This exercise encourages students to identify the core meaning of the present perfect by contrasting it with present simple and past simple.

1 Ask students to work together to categorize the sentences and phrases. Check as a class.

Answers

1 a
2 c
3 a
4 b
5 c

2 Establish which phrases are present perfect and how this is formed.

Answers

2 and 5 Present perfect

There is a grammar reference and exercise on the present perfect vs. past simple on page 153 of the Student's Book.

There is also further practice of this language in the photocopiable exercise on page 122.

Reading p104

1 Elicit which product they think was invented first and last. Do not tell them the answers yet but ask them to match products and dates (encourage guesswork!) and then briefly compare their answers with their partner.

Answers

1 1926 Pop-up toaster
2 1979 Cellular phone
3 1956 Pager (in 1955, it introduced the 'batwing ' M.)
4 1964 Tape recorder

2 Ask students individually to rank all the inventions from the most to the least useful. Ensure they understand *transistor radio*. This activity should help clarify any words not understood as well as being a useful lead in to the topic.

3 Now students should work with a partner, compare their lists and justify their own ranking.

Skimming and scanning

4 Tell students that they are now going to find out more about the products mentioned in the Lead in and that they have to match each product to one of the statements. Set a time limit of about eight minutes in order to improve reading speed and emphasize that this is vital in the IELTS Reading module.

Answers

0 Transistor radio (*Seventy-four per cent of Japanese homes had a radio in the mid-Fifties ...*)
1 Bush TV (*Legend has it that many of these obsolete TVs were ... turned into fish tanks.*)
2 Pop-up toaster (*... toasters didn't really catch on in Europe until the 1950s.*)
3 Tape recorder (*... the TC-100 was less than half the weight of the lightest reel-to-reel and took half the space.*)
4 Pager (*... hospitals immediately adopted it.*)
5 Computer mouse (*... was born of research ... conducted during World War Two.*)
6 Cellular phone (*... functions not only as a phone but also as a fax, calculator ...*)

True, False and Not Given

5 Remind students to scan the passage for key words and then read those sections carefully. In the feedback slot, confirm exactly where students obtained their answers. Pay particular attention to the NOT GIVEN answers (3 and 8), as students often find these the most difficult to understand.

Answers

1 FALSE (Pager – the trade mark was already better recognized than the company name)
2 TRUE (Bush TV – *After the war, the television ... began its ascent.*)
3 NOT GIVEN (Cellular phone – we only know it was developed then)
4 FALSE (Tape recorder – Sony was too)
5 TRUE (Pop-up toaster – a regular feature in the 1930s)
6 TRUE (Computer mouse – beginning of last paragraph)
7 FALSE (Bush TV – the first televisions were larger, taking up half the living room)
8 NOT GIVEN (Transistor radio – we only know they were popular in Japan)

Aim
The following two sections provide examples of three different ways data is depicted and also illustrate the type of language used in IELTS Writing Task 1.

1 Before listening to the text ask students to think about significant changes that have occurred in terms of buying and selling music over the last 30 years. Students do not need to produce detailed responses but in terms of formats (eg records, CDs, mini-discs, IPODS, etc.), they should be able to come up with some ideas. Refer students to the graph axes and check that they are clear what the vertical axis (sales in billions of dollars) and horizontal axis (years) represent.

2 32 Students listen to the first part of the talk and draw the line on the graph. Elicit what is already shown on the graph first, as an example. After listening they can compare their graph with a partner's.

Answers

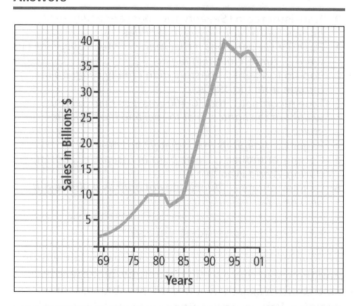

 32

Today, I'm going to briefly outline the trends in world music sales from the late sixties to the present day, as shown on this graph. From 1969 to 1978, there was a steady rise in sales from about $2 billion to $10 billion. This increase was caused by new developments such as the introduction of stereo LPs and later audio cassettes. From 1978 to 1980 sales remained steady but in 1981 there was a slight drop in sales to about $8 billion. This probably resulted from the global economic downturn. By 1984, figures were around the $10 billion mark again. After this date there was a sharp increase in world music sales, which reached a peak of $40 billion in 1993. This was largely due to the introduction of the CD. America, in particular, experienced a tremendous growth in sales but other European countries, for example Britain and Germany, also sold millions of CDs.

Surprisingly, sales dropped slightly in the nineties. By 1996 world music sales were about $37 billion. The following year there was a slight rise but after this sales decreased and in 2001 they dropped to $34 billion. These fluctuations are probably a result of free or cheap music being downloadable from the Internet. It may also be connected to the increased availability of hardware to copy music, for instance, CD burners.

From the information shown on the graph, it can be concluded that ...

3 33 In the second part, they have to fill in the missing information on the pie chart. Before listening they should look at the pie chart to predict the type of answers required, ie formats and percentage figures.

Answers

a) CDs
b) 21.8%
c) singles
d) 0.4%
e) mini-discs

 33

Now if you could look at the following data: this pie chart shows that in the year 2000 CDs dominated the market and accounted for 67.7% of sales. Cassettes still had a healthy slice of the market with 21.8% and singles made up 10.1%. In terms of LPs, the percentage was 0.4% and sales of mini-discs produced an even lower figure of 0.02%, an amount that is likely to increase in the future. In fact, there may well be new formats to take into account. From the data shown on this pie chart, it is clear that ...

4 34 Draw students' attention to the bar charts in figures 3 and 4. Identify what they represent. Ask students to listen to the recording and complete the missing information in the diagrams.

Answers

a) USA
b) W. Europe
c) Japan
d) China

Bar chart 2

a) W. Europe
b) Japan
c) USA

After doing the exercises, look at the tapescripts on page 173 and ask students to underline useful language from them.

34

The bar chart illustrates the percentage of Internet and mobile phone users in different regions of the world by the end of the year 2000. The area with the highest proportion of internet users was <u>the USA with 57%. Western Europe and Japan had similar figures of 27 and 28% respectively, but in China only 2%</u> of the population were using the Internet.

The proportion of mobile phone users, however, was slightly different. For example, <u>Western Europe had the most owners with 62%, followed by Japan with 46%, while in the United States not even 40% of the population used mobile phones</u>.

Looking at the figures for the whole world, it seems that the percentages were quite low in the year 2000, with only 7% of the people on earth using the internet and 12%, or just over one in ten of the world's population, using mobile phones. There is little doubt that these figures are likely to have changed dramatically by now, especially in countries like China, where the percentage is certain to have risen significantly.

Writing 1 p107

Exemplification

Aim
The following two sections focus briefly on two discrete areas that are important in academic writing: giving examples and drawing conclusions. These activities not only provide appropriate language but also serve to emphasize the importance of producing writing that is coherent.

1 Before reading this section, you could elicit the importance of backing up ideas with supporting evidence or examples in academic contexts. To illustrate this area you could ask students to complete simple sentences to focus on the general area.
You: *CDs can be bought in many different places, for example …*
Students: *shops, airports …*
Students then look at the sentences and key language taken from the listening texts, considering the punctuation, before doing the subsequent exercise.

2 Students select a suitable word or phrase from the box to complete the sentences.

Answers
1 shows
2 As shown
3 such as / for example (*like* is not appropriate here as it is too informal)
4 example, in the case of

Drawing conclusions

3 Emphasize that in most academic writing it is important to draw conclusions from, or sum up the work you have presented or text you have written. Ask students to look at the phrases, then refer back to the diagrams in Listening 2 and complete the sentences using a different stem each time. Students will provide their own conclusions so monitor and give appropriate feedback.

Speaking p108

Suggestion
To add variety to this Part 2 activity you could bring some realia into class, eg camera, walkman, Swiss Army Knife, etc, and give a short talk about that specific object based on the prompts on the card. Alternatively, you could find visuals of different objects or appliances, distribute them and ask each student to do the task relating to the picture they have been given.

1 The students have had quite a bit of input in this unit to help them for the theme of the Part 3 activity and by this stage in the course should be producing reasonably coherent, more extended responses to such questions.

Language focus 2 p109

Countable and uncountable nouns

Aim
This section aims to revise the basic concept of countable and uncountable nouns and the grammatical constraints involved, such as the use of articles, or *much* and *many*. Students are also very likely to have problems identifying whether some words are countable or uncountable, which can lead to a number of errors in their written work. Encourage them to check this when they learn new nouns.

1 Individually or in pairs, ask students to use the examples to complete the grid.

Answers

	countable	uncountable
Can use *a / an*	Yes	No
Can use *the*	Yes	Yes
Can make the noun plural	Yes	No
Need to use a quantifier to specify how much (such as a piece of)	No	Yes
Can use *some*	Yes (if plural)	Yes
Can use *much*	No	Yes
Can use *many*	Yes	No

2 Students look at the nouns in the box. Ensure that they understand all of these words. Ask them to identify whether they are countable or uncountable. Unlike the examples above, this section includes words which many students use incorrectly in terms of whether they are countable or uncountable, often because they are differently used in L1. They are also all words which they should learn as they have a fairly high frequency.

Answers

Countable: advance, fact, toxin, dollar, journey, vehicle, report, machine

Uncountable: advice, pollution, money, transport, knowledge, news, progress, machinery, information, research, travel, politics, equipment

> **Suggestion**
> You could follow up this activity by asking students to provide suitable quantifiers for the uncountable nouns which can be quantified. For example, a piece of research, a means of transport.

3 Ask students to look at the essay title and elicit their opinions. Then ask them to read the extract to find out if the writer largely agrees or disagrees with the statement. Finally, ask them to find the five errors in countable/uncountable nouns and correct them. You could also ask them to notice the linking words and phrases used (*however, Certainly, On the other hand,* etc.) and any useful vocabulary (eg *to have an impact, encourages* (someone) *to do* (something), etc.). This activity provides some practice in using the above uncountable nouns correctly, developing editing skills.

Answers

1 Paragraph 1 – ~~progresses~~ progress
2 Paragraph 2 – ~~transports~~ transport
3 Paragraph 3 – ~~many money~~ much money
4 Paragraph 4 – ~~a travel~~ travel – often confused with journey, which is countable
5 Paragraph 4 – ~~informations~~ information

There is a further error correction exercise for countable/uncountable nouns on page 153 of the Student's Book.

Writing 2 p110

Task 1: Describing how something works

> **Aim**
> This section focuses on describing how something works using information provided in a diagram and is a possible task in IELTS Writing Task 1.

1 Ask students how they would feel about travelling in a hot air balloon or if anyone has had this experience. Elicit any comments on how they might work.

2 Ask students to check any unknown words in their dictionaries.

3 Refer students to the pictures and draw lines from the labels to the relevant parts of the drawing. In pairs, students discuss how a hot air balloon works using the information shown in the diagram. They could then listen to one or two versions open class. Minimal correction is necessary as this is mainly oral preparation for the writing task in phase 7.

Infinitives of purpose

4 Students read the extract and discuss the questions in pairs. Draw attention to infinitives of purpose when checking answers.

Answers

1 Why it is used
2 an infinitive
3 *in order to*
4 insert 'not' before the infinitive (eg, *so as not to, in order not to*)

5 Go through the example with the students first. Elicit from them which words *so as not to* replaces and get students to cross them out. Then ask them use the two expressions from exercise 4 to make the sentences more suitable for academic writing.

Answers

1 Balloons are usually bright colours *so as to / in order to* be easily visible.
2 Many people use mobile phones *so as to / in order to* stay in close contact with friends and colleagues.
3 People use computers *so as to / in order to* get information quickly.
4 The public must use their cars as little as possible *so as not to / in order not to* cause unnecessary pollution and congestion.

6 Ask students to complete the model answer using the diagrams and words and phrases from exercise 2.

Answers

1 steel ropes
2 basket
3 is attached
4 is inflated
5 are determined
6 a safety harness
7 using the blast valve
8 the burner

Writing: further practice

Having completed the previous activities, this task could be set as a timed-writing activity in class or for homework. Give feedback as necessary.

Answer

Sample answer on page 163.

Listening skills p112

Listening and writing simultaneously

Aim
This section gives further practice in listening for specific information and writing notes while listening to a text, both skills that are relevant in all parts of the Listening module. Both texts are similar to Part 2 texts.

1 🔊 35 Refer students to the table so that they know what information to listen for, then play the recording for them to complete the table.

Suggestion
Correct capitalization is important. Ensure students understand that all titles and proper names are capitalized, eg Mr John Smith, and that all words in names of places and book titles are capitalized, except for small words such as prepositions and articles (unless they come at the beginning), eg The National Gallery, *The Impact of the Gold Rush in America*. Subtitles are not usually capitalized.

Answers

All answers require correct capitalization

	Title	Authors
1	Understanding Economic Markets	David Royce
2	Microeconomics: an introduction	Bill Harris and Sarah Tarnley
3	Economics Today	Julie Bond

🔊 35

(T = Tutor; S = Student)

T: OK, if you can just make a note of the following books that you're all expected to have copies of for next term. The first one is by <u>David Royce, that's R.O.Y.C.E. It's called 'Understanding Economic Markets'</u>, and it's by David Royce. This is a really useful book, which covers all the core ideas we explore in the first few weeks. Please make sure you've finished reading 'Understanding Economic Markets' BEFORE the start of term. Then, <u>'Microeconomics: an introduction', by Bill Harris and Sarah Tarnley, T.A.R.N.L.E.Y</u>. As it says, an introduction to microeconomics, so you should find this quite easy to follow, even though the ideas may seem a little complicated at first. Hopefully, your lectures will make things clearer.

S: Sorry, could you repeat the name and authors of the second book, please?

T: Yes, 'Microeconomics: an introduction', by Bill Harris and Sarah Tarnley, that's spelt T.A.R.N.L.E.Y, and Harris is H.A.R.R.I.S. OK? Finally, if you can all also get hold of <u>'Economics Today', by Julie Bond, please. That's Julie with an 'e', J.U.L.I.E, Bond, B.O.N.D. OK?</u>

2 🔊 36 Remind students that they may have to change what they hear, even though there is no word limit here, in order for the notes to make grammatical sense. All answers require correct capitalisation.

Answers

1	Paula		07790 765456
2		results of job interview	01923 7766892
3	Dentist	appointment at 9 am tomorrow	
4	Paula	email her	p.reece@somers.co.uk

🔊 36

(AV = Automated Voice; C1 = Caller 1, etc.)

AV: You have four new messages. First new message, received at 9.29 am today. Beep.

C1: Hi, Steve, this is <u>Paula</u>. I'm in Manchester on business today and I was hoping we could meet for lunch to discuss that new contract. If you get this message in time, could you call me <u>on 07790 765456</u>? That's 07790 765456. Cheers.

AV: Second new message, received at 10.10 am today. Beep.

C2: Mr Wilkes? I don't know if you'll remember me, my name's Joe Fuller. <u>I came in for an interview last week for a job.</u> It's just that I haven't heard anything yet. Would it be at all possible for you to ring me? I'll be at home all day. It's <u>01923 7766892</u>. Thank you very much. Perhaps I'd better say the number again? It's 01923 7766892. Thank you again.

AV: Third new message, received at 11.30 am today. Beep.

C3: This is a message for Stephen Wilkes. We'd just like to remind him that he has an <u>appointment here with the dentist at 9 am tomorrow morning</u>. If there's any problem, he could ring the dental surgery on 01923 4567622.

AV: Fourth new message, received at 3.10 pm today. Beep.

C4: <u>This is Paula again.</u> It's now some time after 3.00 and I need to be getting back, so I'm just ringing to say I guess we'll have to meet up some other time. Never mind. <u>You could email me. My address is p dot reece (R.E.E.C.E.) @ somers (S.O.M.E.R.S.) dot co dot uk.</u> Hope to speak to you soon, one way or the other.

Editing 2

Aim
This exercise aims to consolidate and practise work introduced in the last unit's Study skills section and to emphasize the importance of accuracy in academic writing.

1 Students work together to brainstorm ideas. Encourage them to think about less obvious developments, such as the washing machine, air travel, medical advances, etc. Ensure each group has agreed on the three they feel are most important.

2 Set a time limit of about three to four minutes for students to read the text and compare with their own ideas. Point out that there are some errors in the text, but that they should ignore them at this stage.

Suggestion
Although this text is fairly similar in structure to those given in Task 2 of the IELTS Writing module, candidates would usually be asked to consider a more complex issue than this. It is, however, a useful model to use to point out organization of this kind of answer (eg introduction, conclusion, paragraphs, topic sentences, linking words, etc.,.

3 Students work in pairs to correct identified mistakes and then individually to identify and correct further errors, checking in pairs. Monitor and feedback as a class.

Answers

1 The past hundred years <u>have seen</u> *(tense)* enormous developments in technology. ... <u>Moreover,</u> *(spelling)* they have also driven many dramatic changes in our society.

It <u>could be argued</u> *(tense)* that one of the most important advances ... where contacting someone involved seeing them face to face or writing them <u>a letter</u> *(article)*, which <u>would take</u> *(extra 'be' – a common mistake with Chinese students)* days, or possibly weeks to reach them. Furthermore, in these days of mobile phones, the <u>equipment</u> *(countable / uncountable)* needed to call someone ...

2 ... The majority <u>of</u> *(missing preposition)* people in the developed world ... to easily access <u>news, information</u>, or get <u>advice</u> *(3x count / non count mistakes – these words are commonly difficult for students)* on everything from medical to financial problems.

Another development that has been of great social significance <u>is</u> *(missing verb)* the washing machine. ... With the advent of such labour saving devices, women had more freedom to choose to have a career as well as a family. <u>It is often said</u> *(passive / active)* that this has had a very destabilizing effect on families, but it has also enabled many women to have <u>satisfying</u> *(spelling)* careers, and I feel ...

Although many other advances could be said to be <u>significant</u>, *(word form)* in my opinion these three are the ones which have changed society the most.

As in Unit 1, ensure students understand that these words are useful in academic writing, ie for productive use. Ask them to find the words in the context of the unit before looking them up in a dictionary.

rank (page 104 *Now* **rank** *them in order of usefulness to society.*)
convince (page 105 *After its launch, Sony still had to* **convince** *the public, so it sold transistors to other companies.*)
attribute (page 105 *... although exactly who invented it remains unclear, collective credit is usually* **attributed** *to Swedish giant Ericsson.*)
launch (page 105 *After its* **launch***, Sony still had to convince the public, so it sold transistors to other companies.*)
simultaneously (page 105 *If trannies appeared* **simultaneously** *under the Matsushita and Sanyo companies ...*)
credit (page 105 *... although exactly who invented it remains unclear, collective* **credit** *is usually attributed to Swedish giant Ericsson.*)
enable (page 109 *Modern technology* **enables** *people to travel further and faster ...*)
significance (page 113 *Brainstorm what you think have been the three most* **significant** *technological developments.*)
access (page 113 *... can use the Internet and email to easily* **access** *news, ...*)

There is an exercise on spelling words from this unit on page 158 of the Student's Book.

The writing on the wall

Stick groups of three words from this unit and from the vocabulary box on the walls around the room. Put students into pairs, and stand each pair next to a group of three words. They should check that they both understand the three words by explaining them to each other, giving example sentences, etc. After about one minute, give a signal (a handclap / a whistle, etc) for pairs of students move clockwise around the room to the next set of three words. Repeat until the students are back in their original places. You can ask students to make a note of the words they didn't remember, and these can either be reviewed in class, or given as homework to be learnt.

Content overview

Themes

This unit is based on the theme of computing and includes sections on a new software programme and the website FriendsReunited. It also focuses on Internet usage and future developments in information technology.

Exam related activities

Reading

Multiple choice
Note completion
Classification

Writing

Task 2 Analysing the question
Brainstorming ideas
Balancing your argument

Listening

Part 3 Table completion
Flow chart
Multiple choice

Speaking

Part 2 Discussing school memories
Emails and letters

Part 3 Discussing the future of the Internet

Language development

Language focus and Vocabulary

Expressing the future: predictions and intentions
Prefixes

Skills development

Reading
Prediction

Pronunciation

Stress patterns

Study skills

Recording vocabulary

Dictionary focus

Depending on the access your students have to the Internet, you could begin by writing the names of the following websites on the board (with/or without descriptions). They include two (Google and FriendsReunited) which are mentioned in texts in this unit. Ask students to discuss if they have used them, of if they would like to, and about other websites they do use.
Google: a very powerful search engine, which helps you find other websites.
Ebay: an online auction where you can buy and sell almost anything.
FriendsReunited: a school database to help you find old school friends and remember your school memories.
Dave's ESL Café: a resource for English language students and teachers, with chat rooms, vocabulary and grammar exercises, quizzes, etc.

Netdoctor: a site where you can find information and advice on health problems.
Amazon: an online shop for buying books, music, videos and other products.

Reading p114

Prediction

1 Look at the first paragraph of the text together and ask students to exchange their opinions in pairs. Feedback with the class.

2 Now ask students to read the rest of the text.

Multiple choice

3 Look at the multiple choice questions together and check students understand that they have to choose more than one option. Check they understand key vocabulary in the questions and direct them to the glossary. Then ask them to read the text to answer the first set of questions.

Answers

1–3
A (Paragraph C: *we muddle the timing of events.*)
C (Paragraph D: *In a giant shoebox ... it's hard to find what you're looking for.*)
D (Paragraph D: *Remembering what we have, let alone finding it, becomes a major headache.*)
4 and 5
B (Paragraph F: *The privacy and corporate security risks are clear.*)
D (Paragraph G: *the system takes up a huge amount of memory.*)

Note completion

4 Remind students that they should read the summary carefully and find words in the passage which make sense and work grammatically.

Answers

1 everything he can
2 reads
3 phone conversations
4 dates
5 a friend's name.

Classification

5 Look at the strategy box with the students. Then ask them to find the answers in the text.

Answers

1 C (Paragraph J: *Users will eventually be able to keep every document they read ...*)
2 B (Paragraph J: *Bell believes that for some people, especially those with memory problems ...*)
3 B (Paragraph J: *... in a way not possible with the familiar but disparate records like photo albums and scrapbooks.*)
4 A (Paragraph K: *Doug de Groot ... says Bell's system could eventually form the basis for 'meet the ancestor' style educational tools ...*)
5 B (Paragraph G: *Bell calculates than within five years, a 1000-gigabyte hard drive will cost less ...*)

Language focus p117

Expressing the future: predictions and intentions

Aim
This is the second section in the book on ways of expressing the future. The phrases taken from the text include lexical ways of talking about the future (eg *aim* to) as well as the more commonly taught *will*, *may* and *could*.

1 Ask students to look at the sentences and establish that they are all ways of talking about the future.

2 Now ask students to work together to try to classify them as a prediction or possibility, or an intention or plan. When checking the answers point out how the use of another modal verb, rather than *will* can have the effect of making the possibility seem less likely.

Answers

1 B 2 B 3 B 4 A 5 A 6 A 7 A

3 Elicit ideas from the students. They should notice that all the A sentences use a modal + bare infinitive, while all the B sentences use a present continuous form + full infinitive.

4 Students work individually to complete the sentences. These are the kind of topics students may be asked about in Part 1 of the Speaking module, so it will be useful for them to develop different ways of doing so.

5 In pairs, students should find out about their partner's plans. Elicit feedback from the whole class. The report stage provides further practice of the different exponents.

There is a further exercise on expressing the future on page 154 of the Student's Book.

Vocabulary p118

Prefixes

1 Use this question to elicit that certain prefixes carry a negative meaning. Point out to students that prefixes often carry a specific meaning, which can be very useful when trying to guess what a word means.

Answer

They have the negative prefixes in *im-*, *un-* and *–in.*

2 Students write the prefixes then think of examples for them. Watch out for words which begin with these letters but not the actual prefix (eg *missile*).

Answers

dis-	not, or to reverse an action	disloyal, disappear
re-	again, or back	reprint, reverse
trans-	across	transatlantic, transport
anti-	against	antibiotic, anticlockwise
mis-	wrong or badly	misunderstand, misspelt
il-	not (with some words beginning with l)	Illegal, Illiterate (but note: disloyal)
pre-	before	pre-war, premature
micro-	small	microscope, micrometer

3 Working in pairs or small groups, ask students to try and guess the meanings of each prefix. If they find this difficult you could give them examples that might help: *monolingual, unique, binoculars, triangle, quarter, decimal.* Also mention that cent means 100, kilo means 1,000 and milli can mean 1,000 (eg a million) or more often $\frac{1}{1000}$ (eg a millimetre, a milligram).

Answers

1 uni-
2 bi-
3 tri-
4 qua-
10 dec-

There are further exercises on prefix and suffix use on page 159 of the Student's Book.

4 Students should be able to make a good guess at the meanings of the words by looking at the prefix. They can check their answers in a dictionary and see at the same time how many other words begin the same way.

Answers

a) a bicycle with a single wheel
b) to manage something badly
c) the science that deals with very small living things
d) a railway system in which trains travel on a single track
e) something which is already wrapped or in a box when you buy it
f) across several different countries

Speaking 1 p118

1 This lead in introduces the topic in the following listening text, which is based on the website 'Friends Reunited'. Students think about a school they have attended – primary, secondary, college, language school, etc. Using the questions as a basis, ask them to describe their previous experiences at school to their partner in as much detail as possible. Other ideas that could also be explored could be school trips, good/bad teachers, memorable events or lessons, etc.

LIstening p119

1 🔊 37

Suggestion
This listening contains a variety of question types. Give students time before listening to read the questions, predict answer types and underline key words. You might also like to review strategies for answering table completion, (page 36) multiple choice questions (page 54) and flow chart (page 55).

Explain to students that FriendsReunited is a web site that aims to put old friends in contact with each other. Students look at the table and predict answer types based on the other information in the table. Note that in these questions, no more than TWO words are required for each answer.

2 Students read the flow chart and predict answer types and word class. Look at the instructions – here up to THREE words are acceptable. Then listen to the recording and answer questions 1–6.

Answers

1 (a) journalist
2 Mark (NOT mark)
3 friendship
4 former name (maiden name would also be acceptable)
5 workplace
6 £7.50

🔊 37

(G = Graham; J = Julie; M = Mark)

G: ... there have been a lot of interesting sites that have come up on the Internet, recently, but one of the ones that's getting a lot of publicity is one called 'FriendsReunited'. The idea, like all good ones, is very simple – it's essentially a database of schools that you can add your name to and contact other people who went to the same place – people you've lost contact with accidentally or otherwise. This morning in the studio, I have two guests: Julie McDonald, a journalist who has been looking at the site for us, Good morning to you, Julie and welcome to the programme, and Dr Mark Jones, a psychologist who has done several studies into how and why we form and maintain friendships. It's nice to see you again, Mark. Julie, can you start by telling us a bit about the site?

J: Yes, Graham. It's actually quite compulsive. I hadn't really expected to be very interested by it, but it's amazing how seeing a few familiar names can change that – it took me back to my teenage years so easily – I stayed on the site for about an hour looking up old friends. The site itself is fairly straightforward – you have to log in, which just really means giving a few details such as your email address, and your name. Of course, you have to <u>give your former name</u>, too (the one you were known by in school) if you've got a different name now. You might have got married, for example, and people wouldn't recognize your new name. Then, if you want to, you can also write a short note about what you're doing at the moment, what's happened to you since you left school – that kind of thing …

G: Do most people do that?

J: No, actually a lot of people don't bother. It's really annoying, too, when you find someone that you remember and they haven't written anything!

G: So what happens after you've logged in?

J: Well, then you find your school – you can look up your primary school, secondary school, <u>even your workplace</u>. The school part, is great – you find your school, as I said, and then you can look down a list of all the other people who were in your year, or at least, who left in the same year, and access the information that they've provided.

G: And then get in touch with them …

J: Well yeah, but it's at that point that it stops being free.

G: Ahhhh.

J: Well, I guess that they have to make some money out of it somehow and it's not very expensive. <u>You have to pay seven pounds fifty a year</u> and for that you can send unlimited emails to people you know. When I first saw the price, I thought it was for one contact, but it's not, you can contact as many people as you like, so I thought it was pretty reasonable.

G: And did you? Was there anyone there that you knew?

J: Yes, there were – in fact, a lot of names that were familiar, apparently, they have over 5 million registered users, so there were likely to be one or two I recognized, but no, I haven't contacted anyone yet. I can imagine I might do in the future, though.

G: Thank you – and so, Dr Jones, we've heard a bit about this website – can I ask you, what do you think the attraction is of this kind of link up?

3 38 Students listen to the second part and circle the correct answers. Remind students to try to eliminate wrong options and if necessary, rather than leave blanks, to guess the answer.

Answers

7 A
8 C
9 D
10 D
11 A
12 C

 38

(G = Graham; J = Julie; M = Mark)

M: I think that there are probably three main reasons why people are interested in a site like this. Julie put her finger on one reason earlier. Curiosity. That plays a big part. The Internet has a very voyeuristic character to it, that can be very attractive – we can see in, but other people can't necessarily see us watching. <u>It's almost the same kind of motivation that makes soap operas so addictive</u> – we have an involvement with the characters because we've seen their history, and so we want to know what happens next, too. On this level, I think it's quite normal and healthy.

G: So you think there are other ways in which it isn't normal and healthy?

M: Well, for some people, those who feel that they've been successful in life, especially if they didn't do very well at school, it can be used to show others what they've done. For example, the businessman who left school with no qualifications, but now has a company worth several million pounds. These kind of people often feel quite insecure and want to prove themselves.

G: Is this a bad thing?

M: No, it doesn't have to be, but it is important for people to understand <u>that other people's opinions of them aren't so important.</u>

J: It's difficult though, isn't it? We all like other people to think we are successful.

M: Yes, of course, and that's OK as long as it doesn't become too necessary.

G: And are there any other ways that the site could be a bad thing?

M: Yes, in fact, <u>the biggest problem I think it could cause is for people who have not been successful</u> or even particularly happy in their adult lives. These people may look back nostalgically and think that everything was perfect when they were at school.

G: Mmm, looking back can be a dangerous thing, can't it?

M: It can be. It's easy, for example, to think that the girlfriend or boyfriend that you had was perfect, for example, and compare them to your husband or wife now, <u>especially if you're not very happy with your current partner</u>. The truth is that life was probably just much easier then – no bills, no job, not so much responsibility.

G: So do you think this kind of website is a bad thing?

M: No, of course not – <u>for most people it's harmless fun</u>, but it is worth realizing the possible down sides, too, for some people. If it's a bit of curiosity that's motivating you, fine, <u>but if you're at a particularly insecure part of your life, then be aware that this might not help.</u>

G: Well, I'm not feeling very insecure, so I'm going straight home to log on to my computer and see who I can find! Thank you to my guests. Join us again next week for …

Speaking 2 p120

1 After the listening activities give the class the opportunity to discuss these questions, clarifying the following vocabulary item if necessary. Check they understand the meaning of *nostalgia*.

Seek feedback from the class and then tell them to fill in the short form, encouraging them to write clearly. If done anonymously on pieces of paper, these could be attached to the walls by the teacher and students could go round reading the descriptions and then decide who they would contact from the information supplied and why.

Pronunciation p121

Stress patterns

1 This exercise considers words in the same family in which stress patterns change with word form. Ensure students understand that this is not very common, but it is important to be aware of it. You might want to remind students of the work they did on word stress in Unit 6. Ask them to identify which word is stressed differently. The answer, *qualification*, follows the pattern identified on page 75.

> **Suggestion**
> In these examples, both primary and secondary stress is marked. You may want to tell your students that although they will see both marked on longer words in a dictionary, primary stress (marked above the word) is the most important for them.

2 These are all words from the listening. This is another good opportunity to ask students to use a mono-lingual learner's dictionary – they can check meaning if they are unsure of this at the same time as checking the stress patterns. You could also use this exercise to raise awareness of word family building in general, using a good dictionary. You could draw attention to the fact that the initial *a* in the final example (*addictive/addict*) changes its pronunciation due to the stress change, from a weak /ə/ to a strong /æ/. (See also Pronunciation in Unit 12.)

Answers

responsible (oOoo)	responsibility (oooOoo)
curious (Ooo)	curiosity (ooOoo)
addictive (oOo)	addict (Oo)

1 Start by focussing on the visual and give the group a few minutes to suggest the possible content of the letter the man is reading. Ask students a few general questions on this theme before doing the task, eg *How often do you receive letters? How often do you write letters? How many emails do you send/receive a day on average?*

Students do the Part 2 activity with a partner. For feedback, get a strong student to give their response and comment on it.

The Part 3 section gives students the chance to practise using future forms and express predictions about this topic. Draw attention to possible structures to use in the boxes. After the first exchange students could join another pair to discuss the topics in more detail and then report back to the class on the group's most interesting ideas. This activity should be monitored carefully in order to offer an error correction slot afterwards based on future forms.

Writing p122

Task 2: Analysing the question

> **Aim**
> This section emphasizes the importance of reading the question carefully in order to understand the task and then present a balanced viewpoint in the essay.

1 Students underline key words they think are important. You may wish to impose a limit of about six minutes, and then they can compare their choice with their partner's. Students may find it difficult to actually pick out the elements of the statement they have to respond to.

Answers

- Information Technology – there is a specific topic
- The past and present could be mentioned briefly but the main aim is to predict future developments in this field
- Individual ideas and opinions are important

Brainstorming ideas

Students often have difficulty in generating ideas for Part 2 essays. Encourage them in pairs or groups of three to write down three positive and three negative ideas. Further points can be brainstormed and highlighted on the board or an OHT, eg:
Positive: *for educational purposes, work more effectively, etc.*
Negative: *People do less physical exercise, computer viruses, etc.*

Balancing your argument

2.1 After reading the sentences, students decide which writer is more positive about the World Wide Web.

Answer

B is the correct answer.

2.2 Ensure that students have understood that there are two arguments linked together and then ask them to discuss the questions in pairs.

Answers

1. point 2
2. second
3. it
4. but, although, On the other hand, despite:
   The World Wide Web provides useful information, <u>but</u> it is difficult to navigate.
   <u>Although</u> the World Wide Web provides useful information, it is difficult to navigate.
   The World Wide Web provides useful information, <u>although</u> it is difficult to navigate.
   The World Wide Web provides useful information. <u>On the other hand,</u> it is difficult to navigate.
   The World Wide Web provides useful information, <u>despite</u> being difficult to navigate.

2.3 Students can work individually to construct arguments from the ideas they brainstormed, using the step-by-step guide to help them. Encourage them to use as many different linkers and modals as possible. Compare answers in pairs.

Possible answers

It is possible to work more easily from home but there are now more computer viruses attacking systems.
Although it is possible to work more easily from home, there are now more computer viruses attacking systems.

3 With a 'To what extent …' type of question, it is important for students to quickly decide whether they agree or disagree with the statement and why. Point out that answers need to state how much they agree or disagree and for what reasons. Give students a few minutes to give their views on this question to their partner. Invite a few comments.

Exam information
When considering a particular issue, both sides of the argument do not have to be equally balanced, but you do need to show you have given thought to different views of the subject in question. Essays do not always have to have five paragraphs. However, as time is limited in the IELTS Writing Task 2, 4–6 paragraphs is likely to be appropriate.

4 Give students a time limit of three to four minutes to skim read the sample and answer the question.

Answer

The writer agrees with the statement because he/she feels there will be more negative developments in the future (mainly shown in the paragraphs 3 and 4).

Optional activity

Use the sample answer on page 124 to give extra practise in linkers. Ask students to look at the model answer and find examples of conjunctions of:

Contrast: *although/on the one hand, on the other hand*
Reason/result: *as/as a result*
Addition: *also/in addition*

Then ask students to brainstorm other conjunctions with similar meanings and see if they can replace the conjunctions in the text with these alternatives. Note that conjunctions of contrast were dealt with in Unit 5 and reason/result in Unit 6. This will be the first time students have focused on conjunctions showing addition.

Possible answers

Contrast:
In spite of the fact that/Despite the fact that/Even though many more advances are likely …
Many more advances are likely to take place in the future. *However/Nevertheless/Nonetheless*, it is quite possible …
However/Nevertheless/Nonetheless … there are likely to be serious negative effects …

Reason / result
Global communication has become much quicker and cheaper *as/since/because* there is now easier access …
Consequently,/Therefore,/For this reason, … face-to-face communication and social contact will be reduced …

Addition
Moreover,/Furthermore,/What is more, I think computer viruses will be created
Moreover,/Furthermore, What is more, the WWW and email have been used for educational purposes.
The WWW and email communication have been used for educational purposes too

5 This task requires a more detailed analysis of the sample text and will help students see how the writer has organized the text so that both sides of the argument are addressed, giving a more balanced effect overall. Encourage brief notes on key points in each paragraph.

Possible answers

Introduction
Main points: Important advances but not all positive

Paragraph 2
Positive points: Global communication quicker and cheaper
Easier access to more information
WWW and email used in education

Paragraph 3
Negative points: Illegal activities, eg, pornography and information theft
More computer viruses

Paragraph 4
Negative points: More people addicted to 'surfing' and chat lines
Reduces social contact

Conclusion
Main point: Need to consider/minimize negative effects so not controlled by IT technology

There is further practice in evaluating an essay in the photocopiable exercise on page 123.

Study skills p125

Recording vocabulary

1

Aim
How vocabulary is recorded can make a big difference to how easily it is remembered. This exercise is designed to introduce the idea of mind mapping for vocabulary learning.

Ask the students to look at the mind map and the alphabetical list. If students are unfamiliar with mind maps, explain that they set out information so that words which have associations are shown as linked, eg *keyboard*, *mouse* and *monitor* are all linked to *hardware*. Ask them which they think is more memorable.

Suggestion
Ask half of the class to look at the list (and cover up the mind map) and half at the mind map (covering the list) for one minute. Now do some other, unrelated activity for a few minutes (eg some vocabulary recycling from the vocabulary box). Then ask all students to write down all the words they can remember from the list/mind map. Write up the number that each student remembered and find an average for the mind map and the list. Generally, the mind map group will score more highly, and you will have convinced them that this is a useful way of learning.

2　Check they understand all of the vocabulary (eg *spam* is unwanted email, usually advertising) and then ask them to put them into a mind map following the instructions. There is no right answer to this, but ensure

students can justify their reasons for putting words in particular places.

There is an exercise on homonyms relating to computers and IT on page 158 of the Student's Book.

Dictionary focus p125

As in Unit 1, ensure students understand that these words are useful in academic writing, ie, for productive use. Ask them to find the words in the context of the unit before looking them up in a dictionary.

link (page 114 *MyLifeBits can be tagged with a written or spoken commentary and **linked** to other files.*)
secure (page 115 *It may not be very **secure**.*)
chronological (page 115 *Searching for a friend's name would bring up a **chronological** set of files describing when you both did things together …*)
conventional (page 115 *… which THREE of the following are problems with **conventional** ways of storing our memories?*)
generate (page 115 *Doug de Groot, who works on computer **generated** human beings …*)
express (page 116 *Classify the following opinions as **expressed** by …*)
classify (page 116 ***Classify** the following opinions as expressed by …*)
emphasize (page 123 *Does the point that the writer wants to **emphasize** come first or second?*)
locate (page 123 *… it is often difficult to **locate** exactly what you are looking for.*)

Vocabulary recycling

Using mind maps for vocabulary recycling

Choose a lexical set of words from a previous unit, eg from Unit 8, related to health and medicine. Give pairs of students large pieces of paper and ask them to put these words into a mind map, and then use their dictionaries to look up and add other vocabulary to the map. These could be displayed around the classroom.

Content overview

Themes

This unit focuses on the theme of advertising and features advertisements aimed at children and global marketing.

Exam related activities

Reading

Matching visuals with text
Identification of beliefs or arguments
Multiple choice
Matching headings to paragraphs
Note completion
Multiple choice

Writing

Task 2   Review of useful language

Listening

Part 2   Classification
Part 3   Multiple choice

Speaking

Part 3   Discussion on advertising

Language development

Language focus

Modals of obligation and prohibition

Skills development

Study skills

Finding useful language in reading texts

Dictionary focus

Aim
This exercise enables students to develop their ability to relate pictures or diagrams to text. Something they are frequently required to do in IELTS.

1 Ask students to look at the adverts and identify the products and the target audience (in each case children).

2 Before reading the text, ask students to predict how they think the adverts might break the code. Then ask them to read the code and do the matching exercise.

Answers

A 8   B 5   C 3   D 7

You could take this opportunity to pre-teach the phrase 'pester power'. Ask students to discuss the questions in pairs or small groups.

Reading 1   p127

Identification of beliefs or arguments

1 Students identify the beliefs or arguments and who they belong to. Encourage students to find the names or organizations in the text and read around them.

Answers

1   A (Paragraph C: *... by the age of seven or eight they have developed a good understanding of the purpose and intent of advertising ...*)
2   F (Paragraph L: *we see some of the poorest families struggling to keep their heads above water while being bombarded with images of consumption they can ill afford ...*)

3 E (Paragraph A: *they do not understand what advertising is.*)
4 D (Paragraph N: *Children are much easier to reach with advertising*)
5 B (Paragraph G: *if ITV did not have the advertising revenue ... it could not make original children's programmes.*)

Multiple choice

2–5 Give the students a chance to look through the multiple choice questions first, and make sure they have noticed that question 3 asks for three answers. Note that in the exam questions like this may need the students to get all three options correct to gain the point.

Answers

2 A (Paragraph F: *Advertising in the UK ... is conducted responsibly. The ITC's regulations are taken seriously ...*)
3 A (Paragraph G: *... broadcast low cost programmes brought in from the US and elsewhere ...*)
   D and E (Paragraph G: *Quality would suffer and the range of programmes would fall away.*)
4 C (Paragraphs I and J: *The number of advertisements watched by British children ... It's not surprising with statistics like these that the advertising industry is worried ...*)
5 B (Paragraph O: *In the past six years, spending on advertising toys and games during children's television has risen from £26m to £150m.*)

Language focus p130

Modals of obligation and prohibition

1 Check students understand what modal verbs are. Also check that they understand the terms *obligation* and *prohibition*. Ask students to look at the sample sentences and put the modal verbs into the correct category in the table.

Answers

Obligation			Prohibition	
strong	weak	lack of obligation	strong	weak
must	should	do not need to	must not	should not

2 Once you are sure students are clear about the modals above, ask them to do the same task for *have to*, *ought to* and *don't need to*. These are semi-modals, meaning that they have the same function as modals, but do not work the same way grammatically.

Answers

Obligation			Prohibition	
strong	weak	lack of obligation	strong	weak
have to	ought to	don't have to		ought not to

3 Look at the sample modal sentence and elicit that modals are followed by a bare infinitive (ie without *to*). Students should then notice that the semi-modals *need*, *ought*, *have* all need a full infinitive.

4 Students write the modals in the past. This is a complicated area, as choosing the wrong past form can alter the meaning. Check understanding carefully.

Answers

Present time	Past time
should	*should have* + past participle
have to	*had to* + infinitive
must	*had to* + infinitive (*must have done*, would imply deduction, not obligation)
don't need to	*didn't need to* + infinitive or *needn't have* + past participle (in British English, the former doesn't imply whether you actually did it or not, while the latter implies you did do it, although it wasn't necessary)
don't have to	*didn't have to* + infinitive
shouldn't	*shouldn't have* + past participle

5 This exercise presents other useful language for students in talking about obligation and prohibition. Look at the examples, and encourage students to use them in the next exercise.

6 Ask students to write down five rules for their country. In multi-lingual classes, you could ask them to compare the rules in their different countries.

7 ⬛ 39 Depending on your students' listening skills, play the listening twice. Ask them to listen the first time for what was good or could be improved in the student's work. Then ask them to listen and write down the examples they hear of language of obligation/lack of obligation or prohibition.

Answers

... <u>you really should have read</u> the question more carefully.
So, <u>I ought to have given</u> more examples?
... <u>you were also supposed to</u> compare and contrast them ...

I didn't understand that I <u>had to</u> do that
You <u>didn't need to</u> word-process it

📼 39

(S = Student; T = Tutor)

S: Can you explain what the problem was with my assignment on advertising standards?

T: Well, to begin with, <u>you really should have read the question more carefully</u>. The question asked you to compare and contrast the rules applied by advertising standards agencies around the world and you only wrote about your own country.

S: <u>So, I ought to have given more examples</u>?

T: Yes, and <u>you were also supposed to compare and contrast them</u>, or say how they're different or similar.

S: Oh, <u>I didn't understand that</u> I had to do that. OK. Was that the only problem?

T: I'm afraid your handwriting wasn't very good either. <u>You didn't need to word-process it</u>, but it would have helped me to understand what you wanted to say. Having said all that, you did have some very good ideas about ...

Optional activity

If appropriate, you could ask students to discuss how they think life at university will be different from their current lives, eg *I'll have to work even harder. / I won't need to study so many subjects.*

There is a grammar reference and a further exercise on modals of obligation and prohibition on page 154 of the Student's Book.

Reading 2 p131

1 Go through the instructions with the students, and encourage them to read through the questions (1–13) first. You could also brainstorm what they think the text will be about, from the title.

Matching headings to paragraphs

2 If your students still need the support, pre-teach *launch* and *cultural differences*. As usual, encourage them to look for clues in the text which are related to the headings, and note that the key points are often in the first topic sentence, or sometimes summarized at the end of the paragraph.

Answers

1   Para B – vii (*global standardization is inevitable ... Kellogg ... has been very influential ...*)
2   Para C – ix (*it is considered better business practice ... to change their products from one country to the next. ... The best policy ... is to adapt their product to a particular market.*)
3   Para D – v (*Many high-tech products such as DVD players ... Hollywood films are often seen in the United States weeks or months before ... other countries ...*)
4   Para E – ii (*The advantage for firms is that it is easier to launch in one market at a time. Effort and concentration can be focussed ...*)
5   Para F – viii (*The final consideration ... is to take cultural differences into account*)
6   Para G – iii (*... it must take time to find out about local customs and methods of business operation. Equally important is to ensure that such information is available ...*)
7   Para H – x (*depend on many factors, such as ... the key to marketing success ...*)

Note completion

3 Ask students to read the text again, looking for the information to complete questions 8–11. Ensure the students take time to look at the notes and understand how they are organized and what sort of information they are looking for. Remind them that the words they need are in the text and will be found in the same order as the questions.

Answers

8   broaden their markets (paragraph A)
9   Ford (paragraph C)
10   'sprinkler' (paragraph D)
11   Hollywood / American / US (paragraph D)

Multiple choice

4 These questions should not require students to read the text again, simply to find the evidence for their answers. Remind them that 'the writer concludes' probably means that the information is at the end of the text.

Answers

12 C (Paragraph C: *In terms of the car industry, it would be too expensive for manufacturers to develop and build completely different vehicles for different markets.*)
13 B (Paragraph H: *... the key to marketing success on a global level, is to have sufficient information on how cultural differences are likely to affect the marketing of a product ...*)

Review of useful language

Aims
In this section, students revise useful phrases, linking words and example sentences from the book that will help them develop and improve their academic writing skills.

As a lead in to the writing task, students can discuss the ways different products are advertised in their own countries. If some students are unfamiliar with the lexical items *unethical* and *unacceptable*, elicit whether they are positive or negative and encourage them to guess the general meaning (medical ethics were discussed in Unit 4 so they should be able to do this).

1 Focus on the Task 2 question before working through the strategy stages together as a class. This allows students time to consider their response before putting all these elements together in order to form a well-structured, well-argued essay. Stress that the actual content of a Task 2 answer is important and clear ideas and opinions need to be included.

2 Students select phrases from the box on page 135 so each category contains two examples. Note that some of the language was taken from the reading texts.

Answers

Introducing an essay
In recent years there have been many developments in ...

Sequencing points
Firstly, it is important to consider ...
The final point to consider is ...

Expressing opinions: agreeing with a point
I would accept the view that ...
It is certainly true to say that ...

Expressing opinions: challenging / disagreeing with a point
There is no evidence to suggest that ...
I am unconvinced that ...

Possible results
This might lead to ...
This would have an effect on ...

Giving examples
Taking X as an example ...
To illustrate this point ...

Adding a point
It is not only ... but ...
And there is the issue of ...

Drawing conclusions
After examining the issues it is evident that ...
Overall, it is clear that ...

3 It may be useful to do the Speaking activity that follows before the students actually do the writing task (to provide further vocabulary). Allow 40 minutes for students write an answer to the question. Peer feedback could be encouraged with students checking their partner's answer, using the strategy guide in exercise 1 as a checklist. Good ideas and accurate language could be highlighted on the board.

1 As a lead-in activity, bring in a few striking magazine or newspaper adverts for students to discuss in pairs or as a whole class. Students then do the Part 2 activity in pairs. Check meaning of any unfamiliar words, eg *brand*, *target market*, *billboard*, etc. As feedback, listen to examples and allow further discussion of the topic as necessary.

2 The aim of this activity is to pre-teach terminology students will need for the next listening. Ask them to try to match the descriptions with the methods.

Answers
a) 2
b) 5
c) 4
d) 7
e) 6
f) 8
g) 1
h) 3

The photocopiable exercise on page 124 gives further speaking practice, connected to advertising.

Classification

1 🎧 40 This is a not a typical IELTS listening, but is practice for classification tasks, and sets up the following Part 3 Listening text. Students should look at the questions first and underline key words. Ensure that they understand terms like the anti-advertising method from the previous exercise, and elicit paraphrases for *don't have to pay for it immediately.* – ie *credit*, etc.

Suggestion
Note: when doing questions like this, the best strategy is to read all the statements first (1–5) and then mark off A, B and C against each appropriate one as they are heard, since you cannot answer them in order.

1 B (arguably C as well)
2 A
3 C
4 B
5 C

 40

Advert A

(YC = young child; A = Adult)

YC 1: Um … here's a good idea for you. If you want to set up your own business, you should be at least … um, at least twelve. I think that you can sound grown up on the phone, then you should …

YC 2: I'd set up an office at the top of Mt Everest. I'd set it up in the middle of nowhere, so that I had lots of peace and quiet to get on with my work.

YC 3: My daddy says you have to pay for a lot of taxis when you have a business, but I'm not sure why, cos he's got his own car …

A: For grown-up advice about starting your own business, call the <u>Business Helpline</u> on 0800 501 5001 or <u>visit businesshelp.org</u>. We're here to help you!

Advert B

<u>Interest free credit, and you don't have to pay a penny for a whole year!</u> – that's the fantastic Summer Sale offer at Harold's, but it must end this week. <u>Save up to 70%</u> on lounge, dining and bedroom furniture. You want leather furniture? We've got it! You want beds, carpets and curtains? Look no further! You can spread the cost over three years, without paying a penny in interest and if you spend over £200, you don't even have to pay a deposit. Ask for written details.

There's big savings, no deposit, no payments, no interest and no catch, but you'll have to hurry. The amazing Summer Sale must end at 5pm this Sunday at Harold's, Stratford Rd Shirley and the Kingfisher Centre.

Advert C

(1 = Woman 1; 2 = Woman 2; A = Announcer)

1: What are you up to this weekend?
2: I'm trying to get a washing machine.
1: <u>Ah, so you'll be looking for a 'Super mega deal', then, or a 'Price Slasher', or a 'Red hot Summer Sale'? Or maybe a 'Special £10 off voucher – ask in store for details'?</u>
2: No
A: At Star, we check thousands of prices at other stores every week, so you don't have to. You can rest, safe in the knowledge that our price guarantee is what it says. <u>If you can find the same thing cheaper, we'll match the price AND give you £20 in cash.</u> You can trust us, because we care about prices.
1: What about a Blazing Saver?
2: NO!

Multiple choice

Aims

This is a Part 3 IELTS Listening, a discussion between a lecturer and three students in a seminar situation, and aims to give practice in a variety of different question types. The recording may need to be played twice.

2   41 Students should look at the questions and underline key words. Encourage them to speculate in pairs about the kind of information they are listening for.

6 C
7 D

 41

(T = Tutor; A = Adam; B = Betty; C = Charlie)

T: So, you've all had a chance to study the adverts, who'd like to start us off by talking about the first one?
A: I thought this one was quite interesting. It's not a commercial organization, is it?
T: No, it isn't. <u>It's a government body.</u>
A: So, arguably it's different from the other two, it's not actually selling something, it's offering a service to people.
B: I thought that, too, but when I actually stopped to consider the implications, it's not so different, is it? In the commercial sector and the government sector, the aim of the advert is to persuade. Whether that means persuade people to buy something, or persuade people to use something, isn't very important.
A: That's a good point, but I think there is a difference. It's less difficult to persuade someone to use something if the thing you're offering isn't going to cost them any money. Am I right in thinking that the service is free?
T: Yes, I think that would be a fair assumption, Adam. I do think, though, that you can classify this advert according to the criteria we are looking at. In my opinion, it uses simple information to persuade. It's a service that many people won't have heard of <u>and it's probably unique</u>. They are working on the principle that if they say what they are offering, and make it a little bit entertaining with the children's voices, then that will be enough.
C: Don't you think there's <u>a certain amount of repetition in there, too? They said the name about three times at the end, in quick succession</u>.
A: Yes, but that's the same for almost every ad, isn't it?
C: I guess so. <u>It was certainly true for the second one.</u>
T: Do you think that was the main technique in that case, then?
C: No, the main thrust was definitely the half price/ <u>special offer method</u>. The whole advert was centred around what a great deal you could get, how little it would cost, how you could get interest free credit, etc etc. They mentioned that the offer would finish <u>that Sunday, too</u>. I suppose that making it seem as if you can get a great bargain, but only if you act quickly is a

good way of selling things, too.

T: So, how about the final advert, Betty, can you take us through that one?

B: Yes, this one is quite interesting, especially after the furniture store advert. That was so much about selling a special deal, for a limited time only, and then the last one was completely opposite. I thought it was absolutely fascinating, the way they used language like, 'a blazing saver' or a 'Super mega deal'. We hear this kind of thing on adverts all the time, telling us about how 'absolutely amazing' the product is, but here it was used sarcastically, by <u>a woman who obviously felt very doubtful</u> about these special offers and the language used to sell them. It's almost like putting the advertiser on the same team as the potential buyer – they both dislike the way many products are sold.

A: So you think that kind of ad is very effective?

B: Well, it probably wouldn't work for a long series of adverts – it's kind of like a joke – it wouldn't be funny if you'd heard it too often. I do think, though, that that kind <u>of anti-advertising approach is so different, and still quite unusual</u>, that it makes you listen.

A: And that's what advertisers want, of course.

B: Of course.

T: So, of the three ads, which do you all personally think is the most effective? There's no right or wrong answer, here, I'm just interested in your opinions.

B: I like the last one – it's the only one that was different enough to make me actually listen.

C: Yes, I'd agree – although I don't think any of them were very good. The second one might interest me if I wanted to buy furniture – we usually want to believe what we are told, <u>even if on some level we know it's not true.</u>

A: I actually liked the first one, but I'm not sure if it's fair to compare it with the other two, for the reasons we talked about earlier.

T: OK, good. Right, now can we turn out attention to the next question, then ...

3–4 Remind students to speculate on answer types and especially on the possible word forms to complete the sentences.

Answers

8 and 9 1st and 2nd
10 special offer method
11 that Sunday (not ON Sunday)
12 (very) doubtful (NOT sarcastic – she *is* sarcastic, but cannot *feel* this, as it is a way of speaking)
13 unusual / different
14 not true / untrue / wrong / false / incorrect

Study skills p137

Finding useful language in reading texts

Suggestion
This exercise aims to raise students' awareness of how reading can improve writing, and to encourage them to read extensively outside class. You could refer students back to the Study skills in Unit 5, and build on that.

1 Work through the exercises, with students checking in pairs and recording useful phrases in their vocabulary notebooks.

Answers

Paragraph B: It is widely expected that ...
Paragraph D: There is no serious evidence to suggest that ...
Paragraph E: I am convinced that ...
Paragraph G: But there's another aspect to ...

2 Ask students to check back in the text to find out which one is used. You could also ask the students to make other sentences using the same structure, eg *In order to do well in the IELTS exam, ... it is not only <u>desirable</u> to read a lot, but also <u>necessary</u>.*

Answers

Not only ... but (also) ... gives the second sentences a stronger emphasis.

3 Students add a suitable preposition to each stem.

Answers

Paragraph D: on
Paragraph E: to
Paragraph G: on
Paragraph K: to

Dictionary focus p137

As in Unit 1, ensure students understand that these words are useful in academic writing, ie for productive use. Ask them to find the words in the context of the unit before looking them up in a dictionary.

differentiate (page 126 *...to comprehend the purpose of advertising and* **differentiate** *between it and non-advertising messages.*)

legislation (page 128 In 1991, *Sweden introduced* **legislation** *to ban television advertisements that ...*)

discriminate (page 129 *Advertising helps children to* **discriminate** *and to grow up.*)

ensure (page 129 *As we struggle with the question of how to **ensure** that children see high quality television, ...*)

constantly (page 129 *The ITC's regulations are taken seriously and **constantly** revised.*)

original (page 129 *...'quite simply, it could not make **original** children's programmes.'*)

broaden (page 131 *Consequently, there are tremendous opportunities for businesses to **broaden** their markets into foreign countries.*)

feature (page 131 *The Ford Mondeo was designed with key **features** from different markets ...*)

unethical (page 134 *Some of the methods used in advertising are **unethical** and unacceptable in today's society.*)

Vocabulary recycling

Remembering vocabulary in context

Six of the words in this unit's Dictionary focus are from the text on pages 128–9. After the students have looked up the words and learnt them, perhaps in the next lesson, give them either a copy of the text with these words blanked out, or just the relevant sentences as a gap fill exercise. In pairs, ask them to fill in the missing words. If you want to give them some help, you could supply the six words in random order on the board. If you want to make it more difficult, you could include the other three words from this unit's list as distracters. Alternatively, give no clues at all.

After they have finished, encourage them to look for other words in the paragraphs that they think would be useful. You can ask students to check back in the text for answers themselves.

Content overview

Themes

The final unit in this book focuses on preparation for the IELTS exam and includes general strategies and tips for different skills areas.

Exam related activities

Reading

Y/N/NG
Summary completion
Top tips for the IELTS Reading module

Writing

Task 1   IELTS Task 1 Writing checklist
Task 2   IELTS Task 2 Writing checklist
         Top tips for the IELTS Writing module

Listening

Part 3   Short answers
         Note completion
         Top tips for the IELTS Listening module

Speaking

IELTS Speaking module Parts 1, 2 and 3
Top tips for the IELTS Speaking module

Language development

Language focus and Vocabulary

Collocations – *make* and *do*
Top tips for recording, remembering and using new vocabulary

Skills development

Pronunciation

Schwa in unstressed syllables

Study skills

How to revise effectively

Dictionary focus

Listening p138

1 Ask the students in pairs or threes to brainstorm and make a list of reasons students go overseas.

Possible answers

- because it is difficult to get a university place in their country
- because they wish to broaden their horizons
- because there is a special course they wish to take, which isn't offered in their country
- because they want to improve their English

Feedback some ideas to the class, and then discuss the second question.

Possible answers

- it can increase your self confidence
- it can give you a qualification which may have prestige value in your country
- it will give you fluency in another language
- it will give you insight into another culture, which may be useful, for example, if you are conducting business overseas

2 🔊 42 Elicit that this is a talk from someone who is not British, but who studied in Britain. Encourage students to underline words and phrases to listen for. In the Listening module, they will only have time to do this mentally, but to underline is a good practice for identifying key words.

Example answers

1 <u>Why</u> are the <u>audience visiting</u> the university? (ie not the speaker)
2 What are the speaker's <u>best memories</u> of university about?
3 <u>Where</u> is the speaker <u>from</u>?
4 The speaker says that in his country a <u>degree</u> from a <u>British university</u> helps to get …
5 What <u>subject</u> did the speaker <u>graduate</u> in?
6 After graduating, which <u>organization</u> did the speaker work for <u>in his own country</u>?
7 Having a <u>British degree</u> shows <u>employers</u> that the student is …
8 <u>When</u> did he <u>finish</u> his <u>postgraduate</u> course?

3 This is a Part 3 Listening – practising short answers. Allow students time to look through the questions and predict answer types including the correct word form needed.

Answers

1 An Open Day
2 ~~Special~~ *Social* occasions
3 Pakistan
4 a higher position / a good job
5 Politics (NOT Economics, which he only studied for a year)
6 Ministry of Education (NOT the public sector)
7 flexible / independent / fluent in English / good at English (NOT flexibility / independence / language)
8 last year / the previous year

📻 42

A: Good afternoon. It's very nice to see so many of you <u>here for our Open Day.</u> I hope that you've enjoyed looking around the campus and have been able to get any questions you have about courses answered. We open this afternoon with a short talk from one of our success stories. Ali Khan is a former student of the university who we are very proud of. He is here this afternoon to tell us a little about his career and how his studies here have helped him. I hope that he will be an inspiration to you.

Ali: Thank you very much and good afternoon. It's very nice to be back to visit the university. I have many happy memories of my time here – although <u>I have to admit that the best of these are of social occasions</u> rather than lectures!

<u>I first came from Pakistan</u> eleven years ago to study here. I think that the main reason was the reputation that England has. So many English universities have such a strong reputation for academic excellence and a great academic tradition. Also, to be frank, <u>a good British degree is a passport to a higher position and a good job</u> in Pakistan and it has certainly worked that way for me. I'm quite sure I wouldn't have done so well if I hadn't studied here.

I originally came to the UK wanting to study Economics and did so <u>here for the first year, but then I found that actually I was much more interested in Politics.</u> I never wanted to become a politician, in my country most people think that they are only a step away from criminals, but I was really fascinated by the way that government functions and the effects that this can have on ordinary people. I wish I had realized this earlier, as it cost me a year's study. When you're choosing your field of study, I think that it's very important to balance what you think will make you employable, with what you're interested in. In my case, as my parents were supporting me, the balance also included what they wanted me to do! Luckily, they were very sympathetic!

When I graduated in Politics, I went back to Pakistan and began looking for work in the public sector. As I said, I had no intention of becoming a politician, but I felt as if I wanted to do something positive to help my country to develop. I applied for work in the <u>Ministry of Education.</u> The competition for jobs like this is fierce but the fact that I had a good degree from a well-regarded British university made a huge difference. Partly this was because of the standard of education, but I think that there were other reasons why employers favour graduates who have studied overseas. Language, of course, is a major one. Even in Pakistan, where all educated people speak English and the standard is generally high, if an employer knows that you've studied in English to a tertiary level, it gives them confidence in your abilities. It's not only language, though. To have had the experience of studying overseas gives you a lot of independence and flexibility. You definitely need to be flexible in order to cope with all of the cultural differences of a different country. Employers value that, I think.

So, I got the job I wanted and worked for six years in the Education sector, before coming back to England to get a Masters degree in Development Studies. I was actually sponsored to do this by the Ministry, and <u>when I finished, last year</u>, I went back to take up a new position of Director of a project to improve technical education in one region of the country. It's an important post and a very interesting one. I suppose that it would be too strong to say that I owe it all to this university, but the education I received here has certainly been a major factor in my success.

Top tips for the IELTS Listening module

4 Elicit from students what they find difficult about the IELTS Listening module, and make sure that they are clear about the format, text types, etc. Many of the answers in this listening text are quite 'guessable', but the main aim is to remind them of important strategies.

5 📻 43 Before students listen to the recording, point out that a maximum of three words is allowed. Then play the recording for students to complete the text.

Answers

1 Read the instructions
3 questions carefully
5 a possible answer
6 check your spelling

 43

Well, everyone, your IELTS test is next week, so I just want to give you a few final hints on the Listening module – I know that some of you are a bit worried about that part. Remember that there are four parts to the Listening module, and they get more difficult as they go through, but before each section you'll have a short time to look at the questions. This time is really important to you – the first thing to do is to <u>read the instructions carefully</u> so that you understand the task type – is it a multiple choice, is it a table, how many words can you use in the answer – that kind of thing. As you're doing that you also need to think about trying to predict the context – what do the questions tell you about what you're going to hear? It's not really a good idea to predict answers to questions before you've heard the tape, but something that you can usefully do is <u>to read the questions carefully</u> so that you know the kind of information that is being asked for. For example, is it a place name, or a number, or a date? This is a lot to do in the short time you have, but it'll make listening a lot easier. While you're listening to the tapes, write down your answers as quickly as you can, but while you're writing, stay focussed on the tape. If you don't hear something very well and you're not sure about the answer, <u>try to note down a possible answer</u>. You might be able to guess it later. Finally, in the last 10 minutes, transfer your answers very carefully, making sure that all the numbers match up, and don't hang around – get the answers on the answer paper and then quickly <u>check your spelling</u>. Remember that you'll lose marks unless the spelling is correct.

Collocations

> **Suggestion**
> It is very important that students are encouraged to learn words in context, rather than in isolation. Encourage them to look for similar collocations in texts they read, and to note down common collocations with new words they record.

6 Check that students understand the idea of collocation then ask them to try and guess which words and phrases collocate. They may also use dictionaries.

7 Ask students to find the phrases from exercise 6 in the listening script on page 175.

Answers

List A	List B
field	of study
a strong	reputation
the public	sector
a major	factor
academic	excellence
fierce	competition

Pronunciation p139

Schwa in unstressed syllables

1 Remind students of the work done previously on stressed syllables (Units 6 and 10) and ask them to identify the stress in the words. These should all be known, but students could use a dictionary to check. Point out that all the underlined vowels have the sound /ə/.

Answers

preparation (ooOo) technical (Ooo) presentation (ooOo)
support (oO) university (ooOoo) professional (oOoo)
considered (oOo)

2 Ask students to find the words in the dictionary and mark the stress. Point out that all vowel letters can become weakened to the schwa /ə/, but that a schwa is never heard on stressed syllables. Tell them to do this with other words in their vocabulary notebooks if time permits.

Answers

organizing	Oooo
tertiary	Ooo
politician	ooOo
inspiration	ooOo
audience	Ooo

Reading p139

1 Ask students to tick any statements which are true for them. Some students may be feeling worried about the exam, and will need to be reassured.

Yes, No, Not Given

2 Look at the statements first, then ask students to read the text to find if the statements reflect the views of the writer. Remind them that a statement may be logical, but that does not mean that the writer agrees with it, or that it is to be found in the text.

Answers

1. Yes (*Some* (careers) *may be closed altogether.*)
2. Yes (*The world is teeming with people who have found that to be the case whether they have passed examinations or not.*)
3. No (*Practising what you have to do in the examination room is the key.*)
4. Not Given
5. Yes (*... in comparing yourself with others, you find your performance inadequate ... Other people are largely irrelevant. They do not depend for their success upon your lack of success or vice versa.*)
6. No (*They may become more technical, involve more abstract ideas and concepts, involve you in greater specialization and more specialist jargon. This does not mean they become more difficult.*)
7. No (*Examiners do not expect you to have done so.*)
8. Not Given

Summary completion

3 As students complete the summary, remind them to check that they are using an appropriate part of speech as well as inserting something which makes sense.

Answers

1. reveal
2. disappointed in
3. ability
4. ineffective

Top Tips for the IELTS Reading module

Aim
This activity contains useful advice, as well as providing further practice in using lexical links and reference to see how sentences cohere.

4 Students read the tips, and complete them with the sentences below. Ask students to say which words helped them complete the tips.

Answers

1. E – To improve your reading speed and comprehension you should **read** in English as much as possible. As well as books, try newspapers, websites, magazines, even advertisements (all things you read).
2. B – Don't use your **dictionary** to **check** the **meaning** of every new word. Try to guess the meaning from context if you can.
3. A – **Read the title and the first paragraph** carefully. **Reading the first line** of each paragraph ... These techniques will help you to understand what the text is about.
4. G – You **won't have time** in the exam to **read all of the text** very **thoroughly.** Read the text quickly to locate which section contains an answer and read that section carefully to find it.
5. F – Remember that the **questions** usually follow **the same order** as the text. Answer the questions in order, but if you find ...

The additional sentences are D and H. They also give good advice.

Vocabulary p142

Collocations – make and do

1 This second activity on collocations, focuses on some very common and often confused collocations with *make* and *do*. In pairs ask the students to decide whether the phrases go with *make* or *do* and put in the appropriate column. Then correct as a class.

Answers

Make	Do
money	a course
a list	an experiment
an arrangement	an exercise
a decision	some work
progress	research
a choice	the washing up
a speech	a degree
an appointment	housework
a noise	
a loss	
a mistake	
up your mind	

2 Ask if students have spotted any reasons for the categories. Show that words which collocate with *make* and *do* often have similar basic meanings. Ask students to categorize the collocations by meaning. This should show that words related to money often collocate with *make* and so on. You could also point out that *make* is often used about creative things, such as making a cake.

Answers

Relating to study	Domestic tasks	Relating to money
Do	*Do*	*Make*
a course	the washing up	money
an experiment	housework	a loss
an exercise		
some work	*Make*	
research	a list	
a degree		
Make		
a list		

3 The remaining words are: *an arrangement, a decision, a choice, a speech, an appointment, a noise, a mistake, up your mind* Note that *make progress* can refer to study, but may also relate to work, recovery from illness, etc. Possible ways of categorizing might include the idea that make is used with plans and decisions. But there are no set answers to this activity.

4 Now the students actively use some of these collocations to discuss everyday situations. They should select *make* or *do* in the appropriate form and complete the gaps in the questions.

Answers

1 made
2 making
3 do
4 making
5 do
6 making

5 Students now take it turns to ask their partner the questions in exercise 4 and make a note of answers for class feedback.

Top tips for recording, remembering and using new vocabulary

6 Ask students to choose the correct verb and then compare their answers in pairs, discussing how many of these suggestions they already do, or would like to do.

Answers

1 Set
2 Experiment
3 buy
4 make
5 use
6 revise

There is a further vocabulary exercise on collocations with the word *exam* on page 159 of the Student's Book.

IELTS speaking p143

Aim

In this section, students work through a typical IELTS Speaking test. They practise fluency, grammatical accuracy, vocabulary range and pronunciation, which the examiner will be assessing. Information about possible content and advice on how to approach each section is provided.

1 Part 1

1 Students write down questions on topics (alternative questions can be accepted). Correct as necessary. Emphasize that this section is on familiar topics and therefore should help the candidate relax. For most students this is the easiest section so it gives them the opportunity to start well. See Unit 1 for more practice of this section of the exam.

1 Where do you live?
2 What does your father do?
3 What are you studying?
4 Where do you live now? / Who do you live with now?
5 How do you spend your free time? / What are your interests?
6 What are your plans for the future?

2 Students select the best alternative from the words in italics.

Answers

Part 1 tips

- relaxed and friendly – (this will give a good impression)
- longer answers – (monosyllabic or very short responses are to be avoided)
- clearly giving details – (try and give measured, extended answers)
- It is possible – (students can practise this section quite easily)

3 Students take it in turns to ask their partner the questions they formed in exercise 1 and then give comments on performance. After the pairwork activity, you could get one pair to demonstrate and give feedback accordingly.

2 Part 2

1 Ask for a brief summary of what this section involves. Students select the best alternative from the words in italics.

Answers

- one topic … should be easy to talk about – (they are familiar topics)
- Make some notes or think before you start speaking – (1 minute preparation time is given)
- Organize your reply as it is on the card – (structure is important)
- should – (it is important to include each point)
- 1 minute – (this is the minimum, 2 minutes is about the maximum)
- ask you a simple question – (to round off this section)

2 Students read the instructions on the card related to the theme of this unit and then they have one minute to make notes.

3 Students take it in turns to speak on the topic, then ask one of the questions provided and finally comment on their partner's performance. After the pairwork activity, if possible, ask one person to demonstrate with whole-class feedback.

3 Part 3

1   Students select the best alternative from the words in italics.

Answers

- be related to the topic in the previous section – (the theme is linked)
- general – (rather than personal)
- more extended answers – (good answers will have depth)
- You may need to talk about the past, present and future – (this will depend on the question but all may be possible)
- give opinions on the topic – (a vital ingredient of this section)
- Do not ask the examiner for your band score at the end. – (examiners are not allowed to discuss grades with candidates)

2   Students take it in turns to ask questions from one of the sections and then comment on their partner's performance. After the pairwork activity, if possible, demonstrate with one student and give whole-class feedback.

Top tips for the IELTS Speaking module

If students have not read this section, you could ask them to write down five of their own tips for the Speaking module and then compare them with the list. Alternatively, get them to select their top three in order and then justify their choices.

Writing 1 p145

Task 1

Aim
This section gives an opportunity for students to review and practise the skills necessary to effectively describe data in a typical IELTS Writing Part 1 question. It also provides advice on how to approach this task.

1   Before looking at the data ask the class to predict which parts of the world most overseas students in the UK come from. Then they look at the data and compare their thoughts with the statistics. Draw attention to the time and word limit for this question type. Then work through the checklist with them, grouping the data appropriately, paraphrasing the question and eliciting a general statement about the data that could serve as a first sentence.

Give students 20 minutes to complete the task individually.

2   Highlighting strengths and weaknesses in this type of writing (using an authentic answer by a learner) should help to develop awareness of the most appropriate style and language necessary to get a good grade. Students read the sample answer and work in pairs to answer the questions.

Answers for 1

2   It is important to include the most significant information with reference to specific figures.

Answers for 2

Strengths
Clear and logical
Answers the question
Paragraphs (although this is less important for this type of question)
Generally accurate

Weaknesses
A bit repetitive
Only just long enough (147 words). You could tell students that it is worth writing a little over 150 words (eg 160–170)
Some inaccuracies

Note that in the IELTS Writing exam, this essay would probably be of an acceptable IELTS level.

Aim
This exercise gives practice in editing work and correcting common mistakes.

3   Students refer to the sections marked with Roman numerals in the essay on page 146 and work in pairs to identify and correct the mistakes. If this is difficult, give clues as to the kind of mistake which has been made, eg word missing, tense, etc.

Answers for 1

i	the Middle East (article missing)
ii	similar (spelling)
iii	African (wrong form)
iv	total (wrong word)
v	illustrates (grammar – missing third person *s*)
vi	in (wrong preposition) the (missing article)
vii	number of the students (article misuse)
viii	came (tense.)

Students now go back to the text they produced in exercise 1 and go through the checklist provided.

Answers

See Model answer on page 165.

Writing 2   p147

Task 2

Aim
This section gives students an opportunity to review and practise the skills necessary to effectively answer a typical IELTS Writing Task 2 question. It also provides advice on how to approach this task.

1 Students read the sample task based on the main theme of this unit. Refer them to the checklist on how to approach such a task, perhaps eliciting the rationale for each stage.

2 Evaluating an authentic sample answer on a global level should raise awareness of the key features required in a good Task 2 answer. Students read the sample answer to get an overall impression and then discuss the questions with a partner.

Answers for 1

A   No, not really – This answer does not discuss other ways to achieve or measure success but merely suggests how to become successful. Therefore, it has not satisfactorily fulfilled the task set out in the question.

Elicit or point out the key areas that examiners will be looking for. Then give students the opportunity to analyse and evaluate and this piece of written work. Correcting it will also reinforce the importance of careful checking.

Answers for 2

Strengths
Organization: paragraphs are used, there is an introduction, conclusion and the essay displays logical progression.
Communicative quality: it is fairly easy to follow and understand.

Weaknesses
Ideas and arguments: rather simple and need to be developed.
Sentence structure: there are numerous grammatical errors and a limited range of vocabulary. These are probably the weakest areas.
Length: the essay is too short at 193 words.

Sample errors:
fail (line 1) – Wrong tense (*failed*)
success (line 2) – Wrong form (*successful*)
got (line 3) – Wrong word (*gained / achieved / obtained*)
I think that's a big mistake (line 4) – Style: Too informal (Better to say ... *However, I disagree with this view.*)
must to work (line 5) Grammar – (*must work*)
you must ... brave (line 7) – Missing word: *be*
you will have sometimes problems (line 7) – Word order (*you will sometimes have problems*)

to be the successful businessman (line 8) – Wrong word / grammar (*a*)
do not give up, (line 10) – Punctuation: Full stop after *up* then new sentence *This ...*
particlar (line 12) – Spelling (*particular*)

Point out that in correct use of articles, tenses, word forms and spelling are some of the most common errors in written work and therefore ones for students to look out for especially when checking their own work.

3 This gives further practice of an IELTS Writing Task 2 question. Either do this as a classroom writing activity or set for homework. Bear in mind that the students are familiar with the topic, have had time to consider the task and have seen a sample answer.

The photocopiable exercise on page 125 gives further practice of editing language in Task 2 essays.

Top tips for the IELTS Writing module

Students highlight the general advice for the Writing module by selecting the best alternative from the words in italics.

Answers

1   an academic writing style – (this is more relevant for this type of task)
2   those specific areas – (focus on individual areas of weakness)
3   task – (answering the specific question is important)
4   a little – (5 minutes maximum)
5   appropriate – (quality rather than quantity is important)
6   Leave enough time to check your work carefully – (this is important but two or three minutes should be enough)

Study skills   p149

How to revise effectively

1 Many students find it difficult to identify effective strategies for revising. If they are going to take IELTS in the near future, you could begin by asking them to discuss their revision plans.
Ask the class to look at the picture of the students, and discuss in pairs if any of the problems seem familiar to them. You could ask them to brainstorm some possible solutions before they look at the suggested ones.

2 Now ask students to match the problems with the suggestions.

Answers

1 D   2 A   3 B   4 E   5 F   6 C

Dictionary focus p149

As in Unit 1, ensure students understand that these words are useful in academic writing, ie for productive use. Ask them to find the words in the context of the unit before looking them up in a dictionary.

factor (page 139 *a major factor.*)

status (page 140 *... meaningful status in the eyes of others, ...*)

concept (page 140 *They may become more technical, involve more abstract ideas and concepts, ...*)

irrelevant (page 140 *Other people are largely irrelevant. They do not depend for their success upon your lack of success ...*)

inadequate (page 140 *... in comparing yourself with others, you find your performance inadequate.*)

relative (page 140 *Difficulty is a relative word.*)

strategy (page 141 *... problems are caused by the student's negative attitude, ineffective learning strategies or simply the circumstances of their life at the time.*)

respectively (page 146 *The students from Europe (EC) and from the Far East were the most (37% and 34% respectively.*)

numerous (page 148 *... and that you use appropriate/ numerous linking devices.*)

Vocabulary recycling

Vocabulary box

By this point, your vocabulary box should be quite full. Give out a small pile of words to each group and ask them to divide them into the following groups:

Words I don't remember
Words I understand
Words I understand and know how to use
Words I have used in my writing

You could also ask them to think of ideas for games for recycling vocabulary in class, and play one or two.

Grammar key

1 Have you been to England?
2 Is she living in Hong Kong?
3 Has Peter been to Australia before?
4 What does he write?
5 How did he come to school?
6 Should we eat dinner before we go out?

Unit 2 Subject-verb agreement

1 travel
2 cycle
3 travel
4 uses
5 is
6 has

Unit 2 Present simple vs. present continuous

1

1 The sun rises in the East. – <u>Something that is generally true.</u>
  The sun is rising in the East. – <u>Something that is happening at a specific moment.</u>
2 He lives with his mother. – <u>A regular habitual action.</u>
  He is living with his mother. – <u>A temporary situation.</u>
3 I start work at 9 am. – <u>A regular habitual action.</u>
  I am starting work at 9 am this week. – <u>A temporary situation.</u>
4 I read a lot of books in English – <u>A regular habitual action.</u>
  I am reading a lot of books in English. – <u>A temporary situation.</u>

2

1 Correct
2 Temperature increases with pressure.
3 He knows Toronto very well.
4 Come on. We're waiting for you.
5 I agree with you.
6 Correct

Unit 3 Articles

1 a
2 The
3 the
4 a
5 the
6 a/an
7 The
8 a/the
9 the
10 the
11 the
12 the
13 a/the
14 the
15 a
16 a
17 a
18 an
19 The
20 The
21 a/the

Unit 4 -ing form and infinitives

1 helping
2 learning
3 doing
4 to take
5 studying/to study
6 to lock

Unit 5 Future plans and arrangements

1 going to take
2 going to fail
3 will probably increase
4 I'll do
5 I'll try
6 starts (will start also possible)

Unit 6 Defining relative clauses

1 0
2 whose
3 who
4 0
5 that
6 who

Unit 7 Non-defining relative clauses

1 Oxford University, which is the oldest university in the English-speaking world, took first place in the 'Times Good University Guide 2002'.
2 Nurses, who are not well paid in my country, are vital to the health service.
3 Reflexology, which is dismissed as ineffective by some doctors, is increasing in popularity in the West.
4 Sweden, which was ethnically homogenous until the 1930s, has an active bilingualism policy.
5 The Prime Minister, who has been in office for seven years, has resigned.
6 Email, which is widely available in the UK, has made communication much quicker.

Unit 7 The passive

1 was/has been announced
2 were rescued
3 will probably be used
4 is inspected
5 is currently being developed
6 was directed

Unit 8 Conditionals

1

1 Real
2 Unreal
3 Real
4 Unreal
5 Real
6 Unreal

2

1 Unless the government does something about pollution, our health and our children's health will suffer.
3 The population will continue to grow unless something is done to prevent it.
5 Unless you have been to the immigration office, you should go this afternoon.

Unit 9 Present perfect vs. past simple

1 haven't been
2 have lived
3 graduated
4 studied (in the past) have studied (I'm still there)
5 took
6 has given (just now) gave (in the past)
7 have been (at some point up to now) / went (I won't go again)
8 has lived (he still does) / lived (he used to)

Unit 9 Countable and uncountable nouns

1 I have <u>a pen</u> in my back pocket.
2 There have been a lot of price <u>rises</u> in the last few years.
3 <u>All the advice</u> I get just makes me more confused.
4 I don't have <u>many</u> dollars in cash, but I can write you a cheque.
5 Can you bring my <u>luggage</u>, please?
6 Oh, no! Not more <u>homework</u>!

Unit 10 Expressing the future

1 I aim to finish my studies in a year.
2 (Eventually) I might (eventually) do a PhD (eventually).
3 (Soon) I will (soon) start my new course (soon)*.
4 I would like to work in my father's company some day.
5 I hope to improve my English gradually.
6 I could go home next year, but I probably won't.

* Note possible positions for adverbs of frequency.

Unit 11 Modals of obligation and prohibition, past and present

1 People had to be treated equally regardless of gender.
2 You didn't need to hand in / You needn't have handed in your essay until after the summer.
3 You didn't have to book your train seat in advance.
4 You had to arrive at least an hour before your flight.
5 Higher taxes shouldn't have been imposed on those with lower incomes.
6 People ought not to have thrown litter on the street.

Vocabulary key

Unit 1 Adjectives ending in *-ing* / *-ed*

1 exciting
2 frustrated
3 relaxed
4 bored
5 confused
6 fascinating
7 annoyed
8 interesting
9 shocked
10 disappointed

Unit 1 Noun phrases

1 a slight fall
2 a sharp decrease
3 a slow climb
4 a brief fluctuation

Unit 2 Collocation

1	heavy		lights
	air	TRAFFIC	fumes
			jams
2	main	ROAD	rage
			users
			safety

Unit 3 Synonyms

1

1 expedition
2 drive
3 flight
4 voyage
5 outing
6 tour

2

1 flight
2 crossing
3 an expedition
4 tour
5 journey
6 voyage

Unit 4 Dependent prepositions

1 of
2 with
3 with
4 on
5 into
6 for
7 about
8 for

Unit 5 Suffixes *-ful* and *-less*

Noun / Verb	*-ful*	*-less*
harm	*harmful*	harmless
use	useful	useless
peace	peaceful	–
tact	tactful	*tactless*
skill	skillful	–
home	–	homeless
care	careful	careless
hope	hopeful	hopeless
success	successful	unsuccessful (not using less)
power	powerful	powerless

Unit 6 Collocations

1 crime prevention
2 turn to crime
3 crime wave
4 organized crime
5 crime rate
6 petty crime, serious crime
7 to solve a crime

Unit 7 Verb + noun collocations

1 make
2 do
3 reached
4 go
5 cut
6 take
7 earn
8 puts

Unit 8 Dependent prepositions

1 to
2 from
3 for
4 with
5 for
6 by
7 in

Unit 9 Synonyms

1 manufacture
2 invent, create
3 develop
4 design

Unit 9 Spelling

1 demonstrated
2 Communication
3 developments
4 significant

Unit 10 Homonyms

1

1 b – memory
2 d – drive
3 a – web
4 e – file
5 c – document

Unit 11 Prefixes

1 over
2 re
3 dis
4 micro
5 under
6 well

Unit 11 Suffixes

1 Recognise
2 Scrutinise
3 Revise
4 Indicate
5 Assimilate
6 Discriminate

Unit 12 Collocations

Three similar words

2 sit
3 do

Two opposite words

1 pass
2 fail

Two things an examiner does

1 set
2 mark

Three different types of exams

1 oral
2 practical
3 final

Two phrases where *exam* is used as an adjective

1 paper
2 nerves

Photocopiable pages

A classroom survey

Group A	Group B

Group A

1 Look at the activities you can use a computer for. Choose five of them and interview your classmates to find out which three they do most. Make notes of their answers and find out the most popular activities.

- sending emails to friends
- sending emails to relations
- looking at websites in my own language
- looking at websites in English
- word processing homework/assignments
- using chatrooms
- playing computer games
- watching DVDs/listening to music

2 Write the names of your five activities next to the patterned boxes in the key. Then using the frame, construct a bar chart from the information you have about your classmates activities.

3 Make notes on significant information and interesting findings from your bar chart and present your data orally to a member of the other group.

4 Write a short report (minimum 150 words) describing the information shown in your bar chart. Give your report to your partner to highlight any points that need correcting, and make the necessary corrections.

5 What conclusions can you draw from this data?

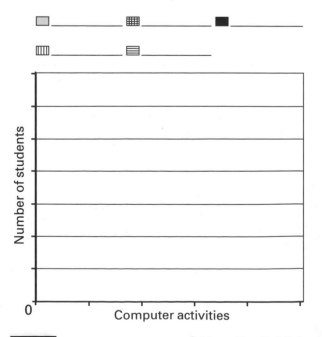

Group B

1 Look at the different types of TV programmes. Choose five of them and interview your classmates to find out which three types they watch most. Make notes of their answers and find out the most popular types of TV programme.

- news programmes
- sports programmes
- soap operas
- documentaries
- films
- cartoons
- music programmes
- quiz shows/gameshows

2 Write the names of your five TV programmes next to the patterned boxes in the key. Then using the frame, construct a bar chart from the information you have about your classmates' activities.

3 Make notes on significant information and interesting findings from your bar chart and present your data orally to a member of the other group.

4 Write a short report (minimum 150 words) describing the information shown in your bar chart. Give your report to your partner to highlight any points that need correcting, and make the necessary corrections.

5 What conclusions can you draw from this data?

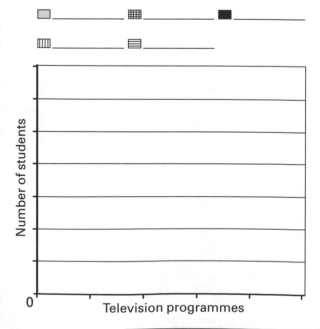

Exploring vocabulary

These words are from the Dictionary focus in unit 2. You could use all of these words in your own essays, but you need to know more about them first. Look at the dictionary entries for the words and answer the questions.

1 What part of speech is *major* in this context?

....

2 What does *major* mean in this context?

....

3 *Major* collocates with nouns which have three basic meanings. What are they? ...., ... and ....

4 Which of these sentences are grammatically correct according to the dictionary entries? Correct the sentences which are wrong.

  a He was forced sign the documents.

  ....

  b She forced him sitting down.

  ....

  c I had to force myself to write the essay.

  ....

  d They forced to him to confess.

  ....

  e The rapid spread of the disease forced the government to change their policy.

  ....

5 Which syllable is stressed in *urban*?

....

6 Which two nouns collocate with *urban*?
.... and ....

7 What is the opposite of *urban*?

....

8 Is *evidence* countable or uncountable?

....

9 What two prepositions can collocate with *evidence*?
.... and ....

10 What two verbs can collocate with *evidence*.
.... and ....

---

major /ˈmeɪdʒə/ adj
1 important, large, or great: *one of the major problems facing our planet* ♦ *The major attraction is a huge clock in the entrance hall.* ♦ *Age is a major factor affecting chances of employment.*

Words often used with major
*Nouns often used with **major** (adj, sense 1)*
■ MAJOR + **drawback, obstacle, problem, setback**: used about problems that are serious
■ MAJOR + **cause, factor, influence, source**: used about factors that are important
■ MAJOR + **change, shake-up, shift, upheaval**: used about changes that have a big effect

---

force /fɔːs/ verb [T]

1 to make someone do something that they do not want to do = COMPEL: **force sb to do sth** *The judge was forced to resign.* ♦ **force yourself to do sth** *Despite the pain, she forced herself to get out of bed.*
2 to use physical force to move something or to move somewhere: *She forced the package through the slot.* ♦ *We had to **force** the windows **open**.*
3 to make something happen: *Opposition to the plans forced a rapid change of policy.*

---

urban /ˈɜːbən/ adj relating to towns and cities = RURAL: *People moved to the urban areas for jobs.* ♦ *Urban poverty is on the increase.*

---

evidence /ˈevɪdəns/ noun [U]
1 facts or physical signs that help to prove something: ***the** historical **evidence for** his theories* ♦ *We are seeing more **evidence of** economic growth.* ♦ **+that** *The study found no evidence that fish feel pain.*

Describing data

1 Look at the table below showing sales figures of DVDs and videos in the UK from 2000–2003.

	2000	**2001**	**2002**	**2003**
DVDs (millions)	22	65	100	140
Videos (millions)	82	72	68	60

Read these sentences and <u>underline</u> the most appropriate word or phrase.

1 The *tallest/most/highest* sales figures for DVDs over this period occurred in 2003.
2 Sales of DVDs (a) *go up/increased/rised* (b) *significantly/dramatic/gradually* from 2000–2003.
3 From 2000 to 2003 sales of videos *went lower/reduced/decreased*.
4 In 2001 sales of DVDs were (a) *slightly/little /much* (b) *higher / lower / bigger* than sales of videos.
5 Between 2001 and 2003 sales of DVDs *more than doubled / increased two times / were twice higher*.

2 Look at the table below about visitors to Australia from four countries.

Country	1991	1993	1995	1997	1999
Korea	n.a.	n.a.	161,000	221,000	100,000
Thailand	34,000	42,000	73,000	62,000	56,000
Indonesia	32,000	61,000	108,000	138,000	82,000
China	n.a.	n.a.	n.a.	64,000	88,000

n.a. means figures not available

Now complete the following short text by filling in the gaps with a suitable expression from the correct answers in exercise 1.

The table shows that visitors to Australia from most of these countries (1) .... in the 1990's although not all the figures were available. Even though visitors from Korea actually (2) .... over this period, it still had the (3) .... number of visitors to Australia of the countries shown. Visitors from Indonesia (4) .... from 32,000 in 1991 to 82,000 at the end of the decade.

In 1999 this figure was (5) .... than the number of visitors from China which stood at 88,000.

3 Write a description of the data in the table which shows the number of visitors to Australia from New Zealand, Japan, Singapore and Malaysia.

Country	1991	1993	1995	1997
New Zealand	412,000	438,000	610,000	641,000
Japan	511,000	641,000	738,000	766,000
Singapore	75,000	130,000	169,000	201,000
Malaysia	43,000	71,000	94,000	126,000

....

....

....

....

....

....

....

....

....

....

....

....

....

....

....

....

PHOTOCOPIABLE

Multiple Intelligences

1 Look at the statements which represent each 'intelligence' and complete them with an appropriate phrasal verb from the box. Use the correct form.

get on	join in	make up	pick up	set up
take in	talk through	work out	write down	

Are any of these statements true about you?

I can .... new skills by copying what other people do.

1 Kinaesthetic

I can .... what's being said in a lecture more easily if there are slides.

2 Visual-Spatial

If I have a problem, I like .... it .... with friends. I enjoy .... group activities in class.

3 Interpersonal

I would like .... my own business or work for myself. I have a few close friends, but I don't .... with everyone.

4 Intrapersonal

If I want to remember something I need .... it .... on paper.

5 Linguistic

I can .... maths sums in my head.

6 Logical-Mathematical

I'm good at .... original tunes or songs.

7 Musical

2 Most of these phrasal verbs are 'separable'. You can say: *I tidied up the desk* or *I tidied the desk up*. Which two phrasal verbs above are NOT separable? Check in your dictionary.

3 Work in pairs. What do you think your partner enjoys or is good at in class? Complete the following statements, *imagining that you are your partner*. Use some of the phrasal verbs from exercise 1, or any suitable verbs. Use the correct form (*ing* or infinitive).

I enjoy ....
I find it easy to ....
I am interested in ....
I would like to ....
I'm good at ....
I particularly dislike ....

4 Now discuss your answers with your partner, and see if your guesses were accurate. Which intelligences do you think you and your partner are strongest in?

PHOTOCOPIABLE

5 A career or a job?

A job interview

1 What advice would you give someone who was going for an important interview?

Do	Don't
• wear smart clothes	• be late
• _____	• _____
• _____	• _____
• _____	• _____

2 Look at these three dialogues. Which person is more likely to get the job? What is wrong with the other candidates' answers?

A

Interviewer: So, why do you want this job?
Candidate: It looks interesting.
Interviewer: And what did you study at university?
Candidate: Marketing.

B

Interviewer: So, why do you want this job?
Candidate: It looks really interesting. I'd like the opportunity to work in a big multi-national company like this. My last job was in a small firm, and I learnt a lot, but I think this would be a more challenging experience for me.
Interviewer: And what did you study at university?
Candidate: Marketing. I did modules in accounting and finance, too, and I enjoyed that, but what I really love is the promotional side of things.

C

Interviewer: So, why do you want this job?
Candidate: I need the money. I'm really badly in debt after three years at university. My bank told me that if I don't reduce my overdraft, they're going to close my account.
Interviewer: And what did you study at university?
Candidate: My degree is in Marketing, but my main interest is music – I play lead guitar in a rock band. It's great.

3 The interviewer asks some more questions. How could you improve these answers?

Interviewer: So what kind of previous work experience have you had?
Candidate: None.
Interviewer: What qualities do you think you have that make you suitable for the job?
Candidate: Ummm. I don't know really.

4 You are interested in the job for business graduates, and have been invited for an interview. Look at the advert. Which of the following might be discussed at the interview?

- your degree
- your family
- your work experience
- your ambitions
- benefits (pay/ holiday/ sick pay/ pensions/etc)
- your hobbies

Dude, you can stop interviewing people now. I'm your man.

Student A

You are an employer interviewing someone for this job. Write down some questions that you want to ask them.

Student B

You are applying for this job, and you really want it. Write notes on what you want to tell your interviewer and any questions you want to ask them about the job.

5 Role-play the interview.

6 Give your partner feedback. Would you give them the job? Why? Why not?

7 Change roles and repeat the interview.

Punishment at school

1 Discuss these questions with your partner:
- What kind of things would you consider bad behaviour at school?
- What punishments were used in your school for bad behaviour?

2 Read the names of different kinds of punishments below and then match each one with its definition.

1	warning	a	being forced to leave school permanently because of bad behaviour
2	corporal punishment	b	telling someone they will be punished if they do something bad again
3	suspension	c	writing a sentence such as *I will not eat in class* many times
4	detention	d	hitting someone
5	writing lines	e	staying at school when the other children have gone home
6	expulsion	f	removing someone from school for a short time

Can you think of any other punishments that are used in schools?

3 In pairs discuss these situations. What kind of punishment do you think they deserve? Why?

a Two fifteen-year-old boys have been caught smoking, which is against school rules. They have just found out that they have failed all of their exams and will have to retake them after the summer holidays.

b Two thirteen-year-old girls were found in the town centre during school hours.

c A sixteen-year-old girl has been accused of bullying a number of younger pupils (aged 11–12). One of the victims is so upset she has missed three weeks of school. The girl accused of bullying has a very aggressive father.

d A fourteen-year-old boy swore at a female teacher after he was told to stop talking so much during a lesson. The boy then threw his books on the floor and left the classroom. His mother has just received a 6 month prison sentence.

e A twelve-year-old girl has persistently arrived between fifteen and twenty minutes late every morning for the last week. When asked why this has happened she blames her mother for not waking her up early enough.

f A fourteen-year-old boy has been caught writing on the back of a toilet door with a marker pen. The door will need to be repainted.

g In a practice test, two fifteen-year-old girls are discovered to be cheating by passing notes to each other between desks. The notes contain important information related to the test. The girls are allowed to complete the test and get high grades.

Giving opinions	Agreeing and disagreeing
I feel/believe that … In my opinion … There is no doubt in my mind that … I tend to think that …	I strongly agree with this view … I disagree with the view that … I do not believe that …

4 In small groups, rank the situations from least to most serious then agree on a final ranking as a class.

The passive

1 Look at the following short paragraph and <u>underline</u> all the examples of passive that you find. Who or what is the main subject of the paragraph? How does this affect the writer's choice of active or passive?

One of the consequences of globalization is that millions of women have been brought into the paid workforce. Twenty years ago they stayed at home to look after their families, now they are employed in farms and factories across the world. Their work is helping to strengthen the economies of their countries, creating wealth. However, the women themselves are often being denied the benefits of this economic growth, as in many areas of the world, they are commonly exploited by their employers.

2 The next paragraph has the same main subject. Choose the best option (active or passive) in each case.

The employers usually employ them / They are usually employed on short term contracts, and therefore have no job security. *The employers force them / These women are forced* to work long hours for little pay. *The employers do not pay most of them / Most of them are not paid* if they are sick, nor *do the employers give them / are they given* any maternity leave. In this way, *global trade is not improving the situation of workers in the developing world / the situation of workers in the developing world is not being improved by global trade*, even though the countries may be getting richer.

3 Who or what are the main subjects of the next two paragraphs? Put the verbs into the correct active or passive form.

The employers cannot really _____ (blame) for this situation, however. They _____ (pressurize) by large multinational companies to deliver their goods quickly and cheaply, and they cannot _____ (expect) to resist this pressure.

Instead, governments must _____ (do) more to improve the laws which protect workers. They may wish to _____ (encourage) trade, but this should not be at the cost of the long term health and happiness of their citizens.

4 Choose two statements from the list below that you agree or disagree with. Discuss in pairs.

Example:

I think global trade should be encouraged because people from poorer countries would benefit from increased job opportunities, as well as …

I don't think global trade should be encouraged because it leads to rich multinational companies exploiting smaller, local businesses …

1 Global trade should be encouraged.
2 Prices in supermarkets should be kept as low as possible.
3 If you are ill, you should be given sick pay until you get better.
4 Smaller companies should be supported more by the government.
5 People should not be expected to work more than 37 hours a week.

5 Write two statements of your own using *should* + passive, as above and discuss them with a new partner.

Our 24/7 store is open on a Saturday?

A debate

1 Below are two statements for debate. Use your dictionary to look up any words you do not understand.

Human cloning is wrong because it is not right to treat a human being at any stage of development as a 'thing' to be used and abused to further the development of science.

Food production must be increased to feed a growing world population and GM animals can significantly help with this.

2 Do you basically agree or disagree with the statements in exercise 1? What evidence or reasons can you give to support your argument? Write brief notes.

....

....

....

....

3 Now turn your notes into sentences, using the phrases below.

Giving Opinions	Agreeing and disagreeing
If you ask me … The point is … Wouldn't you say that …? Don't you agree that …? As I see it …	I couldn't agree more. That's just what I think. That's a very good point. Yes, I suppose that's true, but … Well, you have a point there, but … I see what you mean, but … Perhaps, but don't you think that …
Note that in order to disagree politely in English we usually start by agreeing at least a little and then use *but*.	

4 Discuss either one or both of the questions with your classmates. You should, politely, try to persuade people to agree with your opinion.

PHOTOCOPIABLE

Robot Surgeons

1 Work in pairs. Would you like to be operated on by a robot surgeon? Why/why not?

2 Quickly read the text about an operation carried out by a robot, ignoring the gaps. Was the robot surgeon better than a human one? Why/Why not?

3 Now complete the gaps using either present perfect or past simple.

4 Which two verbs can you find in the text that collocate with operation?

1 .... an operation.

2 .... an operation.

A recent British study (1) .... (demonstrate) that a robot surgeon is more effective than a human surgeon at carrying out a difficult kidney operation. However good the surgeon, human arms can shake when they are carrying out difficult operations on a small piece of tissue or organ. The study demonstrated that robot 'arms' do not have this problem.

Of course, the robot did not work alone. With the help of a computer and highly developed video and phone links, a doctor (2) .... (control) the robot from thousands of miles away.

Scientists (3) .... (already test) the equipment on a plastic dummy. In this experiment, the robot (4) .... (have to) slice through the 'skin' of the dummy and remove kidney stones from a model kidney. Several hundred operations were carried out over a six-month period.

The study, which (5) .... (begin) last Spring and (6) .... (just be complete), analyses the results of the operations which were carried out by robots and compares them with results from the same number of operations conducted by surgeons. The robot (7) .... (be) noticeably more successful than the human surgeons. On most occasions, the robot (8) .... (reach) the kidney stones on the first attempt. Although manufacturers (9) .... (make use of) robots for many years in manufacturing, this is the first time they (10) .... (be) used in this way on people.

Glossary
Kidney: an organ in your body that removes waste liquids.
Kidney stones: small pieces of hard fat that can form inside the kidney.
Organ: a part of your body that does a particular job, eg heart, brain.
Tissue: the substance that animal and plant cells are made of.

Evaluating an essay

In the last 20 years there have been many developments in the field of information technology (IT), for example the World Wide Web and communication by email. However, not all these advances have been positive.

What type of IT developments do you think are likely to occur in the future and what might the negative effects be?

You should write at least 250 words

1 Read the sample student answer to this question. Then answer the questions (a–f).

a Is the writing well-organized?

  • Is there an introduction and a conclusion?
....

  • Are the paragraphs linked? ....

b Does the student copy phrases from the questions in the introduction? ....

c Is the essay the right length? ....

d Is the content relevant? Give examples.

....
....
....

e Does the writer consider both sides of the argument? Give examples.

  Positive ....
....

  Negative ....
....

f Has the writer used an academic style?
  Find three examples of an appropriate phrase.

_____ _____ _____

2 Does the essay contain a range of vocabulary and grammatical structures?
  Find six errors and correct them.

  1 ....
  2 ....
  3 ....
  4 ....
  5 ....
  6 ....

Admittedly, information technology have improved dramatically and changed the way people live in the past two decades. However, some people believe that the future advance of this is more likely to have more unfavorable effects.

Internet is the greatest invention in information technology; it helps human beings connecting each other wherever you are in the world. However, it has some inevitable defects. First, some of the World Wide Web harms the development of young people because it is full of violence and pornography. Some people say that various crimes are caused by young people who see these websites. Secondly, some bad men utilize the Internet to deal in drugs, weapons and so on. Moreover, people's bank or credit card details could be revealed to criminals.

However, it is also an undeniable fact that the IT progress have led to life becoming better and better with more effective communication and it could even save a person's life. For instance, a story was reported that some despairing parents in China wanted to help their baby who had heart disease. If he had no operation for his heart, he wouldn't be able to live longer than five. His parents couldn't afford the huge amount of money and it couldn't be done in China. However, they found a doctor in USA on the Internet and after the operation the baby have cured.

To conclude, although the Internet has some negative side-effects, we should agree that its advantages outweight its disadvantage. Therefore, we should use the law and other methods to handle it properly in order to make full use of information technology and to satisfy the needs of social development.   (276 words)

3 Consider how well they have answered the question by discussing your answers to exercise 1 with a partner.

Chocolate Bar Campaign

The Brief

You have been commissioned by a food company to design, develop and launch a new product onto the market: a chocolate bar The company will select the product which they feel is most likely to be successful and is prepared to spend as much money as necessary to ensure a good launch.

In groups your aim is to 'win' the contract for this snack bar by developing an original product and then designing a poster which highlights its most significant features. You will then present your ideas to the rest of the class using this poster as a visual aid.

1 In groups of three or four consider these points:

- Who is the target market for your product? *age, gender, income*?

- What features will your product have? *taste, ingredients, flavour, shape*?

- Where will your advertising campaign take place? *television, magazines/newspapers, online, billboards*?

- Will it be endorsed by anyone famous? *who, why*?

- Think of a name for your product and give reasons for your choice.

- Think of the design of the wrapper and packaging.

- How much will your product cost?

- Will there be any special offers/free gifts?

2 Design a poster to promote your product to the food company and make up a sales slogan. Then decide which member of your team is going to present which part of your presentation. Remember everyone should contribute to this talk.

3 Give a group presentation to launch your new product. While you are listening to the other presentations do the following:

- Think of an appropriate question to ask the group at the end of each presentation.

- Make a note of one positive aspect of each presentation.

- Decide which chocolate bar you think is the most likely to be successful and vote as a class to see which team would win the contract. You are not allowed to vote for your own product!

Chocolate Bar Campaign				
Name of Company				
Name of product				
Positive aspect of presentation				
Negative aspects of presentation				
The competition winner is				

Editing

1 Read this question.

The increasing number of tests and exams is putting enormous pressure on students and causing unnecessary stress. In many ways it would be more appropriate to reduce the number of exams and offer alternative methods of assessment.

To what extent do you agree with this statement?

2 Look at the sample student answer and choose a word or phrase from the box to replace the words crossed out from a–f.

> For this reason   Furthermore   In my opinion
> Many people consider   To sum up,   There is no doubt

3 Correct the six errors underlined 1–6.

....

....

....

....

....

....

(a) ~~I think lots of people feel~~ that the increasing number of tests and exams puts enormous pressure on students. They are worried about exams all the time and it makes them feel **1** <u>boring</u>. Even though they study hard, sometimes they still don't pass the exam. But sometimes, lots of exams make some students nervous and just some exams decide a person's life.

There are a lot of tests and exams for students. Each subject has different ones. (b) ~~For me~~, so many tests and examinations are unnecessary. But the school and teachers think it is good for students, it can motivate them to work hard and hard.

(c) ~~I know it is definitely true to say~~ that there are other ways that are better than exams. For example, the teachers can let the students know how important to work hard. Everyone **2** <u>know</u> it is very important to work hard. If you don't, you can't earn money, have a good life when you finish **3** <u>the school</u>. (d) ~~Also~~, there is another better way can test students, like continual assessment. Teacher can give some **4** <u>homeworks,</u> or give a few tests, not too often so students will be happy with this way to test **5** <u>themself</u> and they will get better relationship with their teacher. (e) ~~So that means~~ the government must reduce the tests and exams.

(f) ~~To finish~~, there are other ways to test or assess students so they get more free time to practice, more time to do what they like and then more knowledge they will get. It's **6** <u>more fair</u> for most students and make them work harder everyday.

Key to photocopiable exercises

Unit 2
1 adjective
2 important, large or great
3 problem, cause, change
4 a He was forced <u>to</u> sign the documents.
   b She forced him <u>to sit</u> down.
   c Correct.
   d They <u>forced him</u> to confess.
   e Correct.
5 <u>Urban</u>
6 poverty, areas
7 rural
8 uncountable
9 for, of
10 see, find

Unit 3
1
1 highest
2 increased significantly
3 decreased
4 slightly lower
5 more than doubled

2
1 increased significantly
2 decreased
3 highest
4 more than doubled
5 slightly lower

Note: alternative answers may be acceptable

Unit 4
1
1 pick up
2 take in
3 to talk *it* through joining in
4 to set up / get on
5 to write *it* down
6 work out
7 making up

Unit 5
2
B: At an interview it is important to give full answers to questions, either by giving more detail or by giving examples of your experiences.

Unit 7
1
The main subject is the women. The passive is often used to keep the focus on them and on what happens to them.

<u>women have been brought</u> / <u>they are employed</u> / <u>themselves are often being denied</u> / <u>they are commonly exploited</u>.

2
Again the emphasis is on the women. The exception is the last sentence, where the active sounds better because otherwise the first part of the sentence would be too long and complex (the principle of end-weight).

<u>They are usually employed</u> / <u>These women are forced</u> / <u>Most of them are not</u> / *<u>are they given</u> / <u>global trade is not improving the situation of workers in the developing world</u>

*Note inversion after *nor*.

3
The first paragraph focuses on the employers and on what happens to them (hence passive). The second paragraph on governments and on what they should (actively) do.

<u>be blamed</u> / <u>are pressurized</u> / <u>be expected</u> / <u>do</u> / <u>encourage</u>

Unit 9
3
1 has demonstrated (recent news)
2 controlled (during the study)
3 have already tested (non specific time)
4 had to (again on the specific occasions mentioned in 2)
5 began (last Spring)
6 has just been completed (recent news, no specific time)
7 was (in this study, which is now completed)
8 reached (on these occasions)
9 have made use of (started in the past and continues to the present)
10 have been (as above)

4
carry out and *conduct*

Unit 10
1
a Reasonably well-structured: Intro, main body (2 paragraphs) and conclusion. The essay has coherence and there is evidence of logical progression with the argument.
b The introduction has been paraphrased.
c Between 250-280 words: an appropriate length.
d The content is relevant and the answer addresses the question.
e Both sides of the argument are considered:
   Negative – Pornography/violence, drugs/weapons, personal security.
   Positive – Better communication, life-saving example in China.
f Examples of useful phrases:
   … some people believe …, It is an undeniable fact …, To conclude …

2
Reasonable range of structures and vocabulary but also a number of examples of errors to correct.

3
Overall comment: Although grammatical accuracy is not perfect, this would be a satisfactory answer because the essay is well-organized and has a balanced argument backed up with clear examples.

Unit 12
1
a Many people consider
b In my opinion
c There is no doubt
d Furthermore
e For this reason
f To sum up

2
1 bored
2 knows
3 remove article 'the'
4 homework
5 themselves
6 fairer